Traveling with Pain by Liz Hamill is a must read for anyone who enjoys travel. In addition to covering tips on how and why; packing and preparing; getting there; sleeping and eating; sightseeing; outdoor adventures; shopping; night life; resting; recovery time after the trip; Hamill provides a list of resources that any traveler will find useful. Having travelled with pain at different times, as well as being a caregiver, I wish I would have had half these tips. Travelling with Pain will help you make that trip you've always feared you couldn't take, as well as improve those you do take.

> *Maralyn D. Hill*
> *President, International Food Wine & Travel Writers Association*

Insightful and resourceful, Traveling with Pain helps you organize and plan your trip as well as manage your pain within the confines of destination travel. Liz Hamill has an outstanding piece of work, tips and hints even the most seasoned traveler will find enlightening. I am ready to plan my trip and start traveling again, something I have put off because of the pain. Thank you, Liz!

> *Jani Larsen*
> *Regional Director & National Veterans Coordinator,*
> *American Chronic Pain Association*

TRAVELING WITH PAIN

TRAVELING
WITH PAIN

LIZ HAMILL

HUNT PRESS • LOS ANGELES

Published by Hunt Press, Los Angeles, California.

www.huntpress.com

Printed in the United States of America

ISBN 978-0-9790674-6-4

10 9 8 7 6 5 4 3 2 1

FIRST EDITION

Dedication

To Eric, for his quiet, unflagging support through some of the hardest parts of my life, and for always carrying the bags.

Acknowledgement

This book would not have come to be without the help of dozens of people over more than three years. First, thank you to Andrew Stoliar and Catherine Aragon for brainstorming with me on the long drive home from Reno that night—together we came up with the concept that eventually became this book. Further development of the content was assisted by the members of the Chronic_Pain and Endometriosis groups on LiveJournal, so many of whom read my www.travelswithpain.com blog and provided useful feedback. Theresa Mallick-Searle, N.P. provided great information from the other side of the exam table as well as the medical care I needed to finish this book.

Thank you to each and every one of you who's been on a research trip with me—you've all helped more than you know. A special shout-out to my sister, Anne, for using some of her precious vacation time to brave the cruise (and that very long walk) with me.

My love and thanks to my parents, Frank and Diane, for helping to underwrite the research and writing of this book.

And finally to Angela Hunt, my eternal gratitude for your belief in The Imperfect Traveler and your willingness to throw in with me on this project.

Table of Contents

Foreword

The thought of travel can be daunting to someone living with ongoing pain. Images of unpredictable situations, long lines, cramped and uncomfortable seating in planes or cars and the sheer exhaustion of it all could lead an individual with ongoing pain to throw up his or her hands and become a virtual recluse.

Traveling for business or pleasure is often part of a cherished lifestyle. It can be both invigorating and a respite from the daily routine. It can bring loved ones together and reinforce a sense of accomplishment and adventure. For people traveling with pain, however, it can be filled with challenges.

Being an avid traveler myself, I live by the proverb, I travel therefore I am. I have treated patients with chronic pain for many years. Rarely have I stopped to give consideration to how my patients live there lives beyond their monthly doctors appointments. When Elizabeth asked me to read and comment on her new book, *Traveling with Pain*, I was honored and enlightened.

Traveling with Pain is filled with insightful suggestions, pearls, and specifics to realistically plan a safe, comfortable and memorable trip. Be it a weekend away at a local hotel or a month long adventure across the continent, traveling with pain is 90% planning/preparation, 10% implementation and 100% enjoyable.

- Theresa Mallick-Searle
  Nurse Practitioner
  Stanford Medical Center, Division Pain Management

Preface

So who is this imperfect traveler, anyway?

The short answer is: She's me.

I'm a middle-aged woman with chronic, invisible health problems that impact the ways in which I can travel. My biggest problem is constant chronic pelvic pain, which runs the gamut from mild aches to searing pains. I've also got a bladder condition that makes me need to go to the bathroom a lot. If I can't get to the restroom regularly, the pain gets worse. Obviously, these little problems can trip up my trip plans.

So many prominent guidebook series seem to be written only for "perfect" travelers—super-fit, totally healthy people who love to carry all their luggage on their backs, stay up all night swilling beer with other tourists in dorm-style rooms, and sleep five hours per night on third-hand mattresses. These amazing physical specimens think nothing of walking or hiking more than 10 miles each day, don't have to worry about what they eat (or how much), nor do they ever seem to have to go to the bathroom. This perfect traveler would rather wash the same pair of underpants in the hostel sink every single night for a month than be seen carrying an extra suitcase.

Smaller subsets of guidebooks are written for rich people. Got $25,000 to blow on your next vacation? That'll make it lots easier—the average 5-star hotel's got bell service, elevators with sofas in them, and butlers to bring every single thing you want straight to your door. Sadly, I don't have that kind of cash.

The Imperfect Traveler's Guides are for the rest of us—travelers who have chronic health problems, special medical needs or dietary restrictions…pretty much anything physical, mental, or emotional that makes traveling a challenge. The Imperfect Traveler takes your finances into account too.

You don't have to be either rich or physically perfect to take a perfect trip. Whether you want to slip away for a romantic weekend with your sweetie, pack the kids into the car for a classic family vacation, or embark on an ambitious international sabbatical, you can. You just need practice, planning, information, and know-how. That's where The Imperfect Traveler's Guides come in.

Specifically, The Imperfect Traveler's Guide to Traveling with Pain aims to help people with chronic and acute pain to travel more comfortably, more easily, and just plain more. This book covers travel from the first dreams of a destination, through planning and reservations, to climbing aboard your transportation, checking into your lodgings, and heading out on adventures.

Yes, it's harder to travel with pain than without it. I know—I've carted my pain around with me on dozens of trips. But I can't think of anything more worth doing that leaving home, getting out, and exploring the world. Traveling makes me happy—I love to see new things, do new things, and to discover places and sights and people I never dreamed of.

I hope this book will help you find your own dreams, and enjoy a multitude of great destinations and vacations.

— Liz Hamill
The original Imperfect Traveler

Chapter 1: How and Why to Travel With Pain

Of all the nonmedical means of treating my chronic illnesses that I've tried, getting out of my house and on the road works best. There's nothing like a vacation or even a business trip to distract me from my pain and fatigue. I might even be getting into a pain groove, my world starting to narrow down to that one spot inside my belly, the sweat breaking out onto my brow, and...oh! It's a llama farm/velodrome/biodynamic winery/whatever. Shiny! Pain all gone, or at least mostly forgotten.

In Europe, the standard vacation time allotted to workers is 6 weeks per year. That's a lot of why you see all those smiling, relaxed looking topless ladies in photos of the French and Italian and Spanish Rivieras. They've had time to really chill out and get mellow. To get that same look, join them on vacation! They'll let you go topless too (if that's your pleasure), and many of the French Riviera beaches and boardwalks are very flat and easily accessible regardless of your fatigue or mobility levels. Once you're situated under an umbrella on the sand overlooking the Mediterranean, you can just go to sleep.

The moral of this story: those of us with chronic disabilities have a lot of base stress and unpleasantness in our lives. The more stuff we can do to make ourselves happy, the better off we'll be both emotionally and physically. Going on vacation makes most people happy. Pain patients doubly so, because we're off our couches, out of our homes, and doing something normal and positive and fun. The boost I get from feeling capable of travel, regardless of how limited the scope of my activities, makes me feel fabulous. It makes me feel like a real person again.

In addition to helping you feel better, a quick weekend getaway or a four-week safari in Africa on your part can provide a much-needed respite for your primary caregiver, even if you take him or her with you. You get a nap in a comfy hotel bed every afternoon, and your caregiver gets a hike in a park, a stroll through a museum, or a long lunch in a meat-heavy restaurant. You go to bed early one night, and your partner gets to go out to investigate the local bar or club scene.

Possibly better still, you might ask a friend or family member who's not your primary caregiver (but knows you, your needs, and your routine) to travel with you. If you can, offer to pay for part of the trip and you might find your loved ones vying for the chance to carry your luggage and stop for the bathroom every 30 minutes. This tactic gives your primary caregiver a real, honest-to-goodness break.

Don't have a partner to travel with to that exotic foreign destination you've always wanted to see? You can rent one!

There are two rules of traveling with chronic pain:

1. Plan as much as you can in advance of your trip.
2. Expect that at least half your plans will fall through, fail, or blow up.

Come to think of it, those rules work pretty well for travelers of all ability levels.

Setting Reasonable Expectations
Or, Why Your First Trip in 10 Years Shouldn't Be To Outer Mongolia

Have you been lying on your couch for the last five years, unable or unwilling to leave your home or hometown due to a serious medical condition? Then put the guidebook to Siberian backpacking adventures down and slowly back away.

You're not ready. And the hard, cold truth is that you may never be ready for the kind of exotic trip that adventure writers rave about. Neither might I, and I am travel writer. But before you give up on ever leaving home again, take a moment. Think about why you'd *want* to camp in wintertime Siberia, trek across mine-pocked deserts in Sudan, or climb grimy tree-free mountains in Uzbekistan. Do these things really sound like fun? At all? Do your healthy friends go on trips like this?

It's wonderful to aspire to see the pyramids of Egypt from the back of a camel, walk along the Great Wall of China, and bathe in the hot springs of Chile. Those hot springs might be just the right therapy for all kinds of chronic pain. As for Sudan and Siberia and Saudi Arabia—some places are better to experience only through the writings of big, bluff, brimming-with-health travel writers. (Who aren't me.)

But you're not going to make it to Egypt if you don't first "practice" to build up your traveling muscles (physical, mental, and emotional). Like any other activity, traveling with chronic pain gets easier with practice. By taking shorter, easier trips at first, you build up endurance and experience, so that when you try a longer excursion you don't fail, wreck your precarious health, and wind up in bed for a month.

The First Grand Adventure: One Night in a Motel

For your first trip with chronic pain, plan only one night away from home. After years of battling my body and spending my gas money on doctor's visits, one of my favorite vacations is a weekend at an inexpensive but clean chain motel located less than an hour from my house.

Got a beach nearby? How about a picturesque lake? Forest? Desert? Pile of rocks? Maybe a small town with good antique stores, or a big city with fabulous food? Wherever you live, find an intriguing place to visit that's less than two hour's drive from your house. The less travel time, the less physical strain, the more fun the vacation.

Find the comfiest accommodations your budget can bear. (Remember, you're saving up for bigger and better trips now too!) If you can afford a room at a Four Seasons or a Fairmont, snap it up! Now *is* the time to indulge yourself with a massage, complimentary wine and cheese, some time in a hot tub, and 500-thread-count sheets.

Can't afford a five-star spa resort? Do not let that stop you from taking that trip! A mid-priced motel can feel just fine. Even a super-cheap room in a hostel might work, depending on your physical condition and limitations. The point is to change your surroundings, break your patterns, and disrupt your routines. Do something different, even if it's as simple as enjoying the view out of a new set of windows.

After your first overnight trip, keep taking it slow. If one night away feels easy and great, try a weekend. Then a long weekend. As your knowledge of how to care for yourself when you're away from home increases, you'll be able to start taking longer vacations to places farther away.

Traveler's Self-Assessment

How are you feeling these days? Honestly? Here's a quick quiz to help you determine your current State of You:

1.   Can you get out of bed and walk around your house

unaided? _____

2.   Can you use the bathroom without pain?

_____

3.   Can you walk 100 yards comfortably? ½ mile? 1 mile?

More? _____

4.   Do you exercise? Does it feel good or bad?

_____

5.   Have you gone out to eat a restaurant in the last month?

_____

6.   Do you use public transit around your home?

_____

7.   Can you drive a car? (Take into account both pain level and

medications.) _____

8.   Can you comfortably ride in a car with somebody else

driving? For how long? _____

9.   Do you work? Full-time or part-time? From home, or do

you commute? _____

The more yeses you answered and the more active you are at home, the grander your first adventure away from home can be. It's still not a great idea to plan a 10-day class-5 whitewater kayak trip for your first vacation in years. But if you're able to walk a mile and go a couple of hours between bathroom breaks, you might be able to take a shopping expedition, a beachside getaway, or an overnight national park adventure.

Even if you answered no to every single question, you can still take a day off and spend some time away from home. It will just take a little bit more determination and planning.

Reframing Your Expectations: Imagine Your Condition as a Two-Year-Old Child

Focusing on how much pain you're in and the ins and outs of your medical condition doesn't make it easier to plan a trip.

Instead, try this exercise: Think of your condition as if it were a two-year-old child. Millions of parents travel with toddlers every day of every year—it's considered a normal, even desirable thing to do. Consider the following:

- Toddlers require special plans, from choosing the right hotel room to planning special activities to remembering to bring the doctor's phone number along.
- Traveling with a toddler means packing differently and it means lugging special items around throughout your trip.
- Toddlers can't do all the same things adults can—no downhill skiing, no back-country hikes, no 10-hour sojourns in art museums, no all-nighters at the hottest night clubs.
- Toddlers need to eat frequently (and healthfully) and sleep on a regular schedule to keep happy and even-tempered, especially on vacation.

- Despite all the best planning and scheming, sometimes toddlers have tantrums and spoil an outing. It's not fun to have to abandon plans in the middle of the day, but it's not the end of the world either.

Now substitute "chronic pain condition" for "toddler" in each sentence. You'll realize that while traveling with pain can be a pain, it's something you *can* do. At least your pain won't throw food at other diners in a restaurant or start screaming during an opening night performance on Broadway!

Researching Your Dream Vacation

Before you hop in the car and head for the open road, take some time to check out your proposed destination before you check in to your hotel.

When you've got pain, you've got different needs than the average able-bodied traveler. Your specific requirements for hotels, restaurants, and attractions will depend on your condition when you travel—you know your own body best.

- Can you climb stairs easily, even after a long hard day? If not, request a room on the ground floor or be sure that a working elevator will be available.
- Do you need an afternoon nap? Make sure you're not staying in a hostel that has an afternoon "lockout." (Few do this anymore, but it's still best to be sure.)
- Can you walk 100 yards comfortably? If not, ask how far the walk will be from your car to your hotel. Check out the parking situation at any major attractions or restaurants too (especially fancy urban eateries). If valet is available, add those costs (including tips) to your planned expenses.

These three questions are only examples—you'll need to think hard about your own condition and then create your own questions. Then answer them. Your answers will form the list of needs and wants to meet when you're planning your trip.

Making Reservations

To make flight reservations, use the Internet to find price deals and for convenience. Online travel web sites have checkboxes and menus that let travelers select special meals and request wheelchair assistance. The usual options allow for people who travel with their own wheelchairs as well as those who need an airport chair and "driver."

If you have unusual requirements on the airplane, call the airline and speak to a human ticket agent. This increases your odds of getting your needs met, but doesn't guarantee it.

Airline employees can't change, modify, or create exceptions to airport security rules. In the United States, check the TSA web site at www.tsa.gov for current security restrictions. The web site addresses some concerns pertaining to medications, implanted devices, orthopedic shoes, and such. Call 1-866-289-9673 if you don't get the answers you seek on the web site.

Lodging Reservations

For reserving a room with special features, the phone still works best. I like to do the initial research online, then call the hotel and request a better rate than I've seen on the Web. This is especially true for independent inns and motels, though even chain motel desk clerks have a surprising amount of latitude to adjust room rates upon request.

Also, front-desk staff should be able to describe individual rooms in detail—they've actually seen the rooms and know things like the age of the mattresses and what the pillows are made out of. So ask about specific room features you need or want (like no stairs or a bathtub); the reservation agent may be able to match you with the room you'll find most comfortable.

Restaurant Reservations

Eating well is a pleasure that people with chronic pain can still enjoy. Most of the time, you won't need to make restaurant reservations until you've arrived at your destination.

The big exceptions are top restaurants in places like Manhattan, San Francisco, Las Vegas, and California's Wine Country. It's a good bet that if you've seen the owner guest judging on Top Chef, you'll need to make reservations while you're still at home. Diners who want to eat at Thomas Keller's French Laundry in Yountville should get their dining reservations first, and then pick out a place to stay, then make transportation arrangements.

If you'll need special physical or culinary arrangements at the restaurant, call at least 24-48 hours in advance. Describe your needs (a padded chair, a footstool, a gluten-free meal), then make the reservation if the restaurant can accommodate you.

Picking the Perfect Travel Buddy

Traveling is always more fun with a companion, whether you've got pain or not. But unlike healthy travelers for whom a travel buddy is a convenience or a fun choice, a travel buddy can make the difference between a great vacation and a failed trip for a traveler with pain.

Here's a quick quiz to help figure out whether you need a travel buddy. Can you:

1. Carry/roll **all** your luggage for 100 yards or more?

_____

2. Walk up and down a flight of stairs unassisted?

_____

3. Stand in line for an hour without needing to sit down?

_____

4. Maintain reasonable awareness of your surroundings and the people around you? _____

5. Drive safely and legally for an hour or more while taking your pain medication? _____

6. Safely take public transit while taking your pain medication?

_____

7. Think and speak clearly while taking your pain medication?

_____

8. Go without pain medication for 24 hours or more?

_____

Bonus Question: Does your medical practitioner think you should travel alone? _____

If you answered No to any of these questions, you probably need a travel buddy—somebody who can drive, deal with motel clerks, carry bags to and from motel rooms, and assist you when you need help. Your travel buddy needs to know before the trip that he'll be responsible for these things and for any other tasks you can't do when you're in the midst of a pain flare. Be specific and detailed with your buddy in advance about your present health situation and medications, even if he's not your spouse or a family member. The more he knows, the better prepared he'll be to handle any emergencies that crop up. Your travel buddy should have a list of all your medications, the phone numbers of your doctors, and copies of hotel and transit confirmations.

Your job is to be as nice to your travel buddy as possible. She's carrying your bags, doing the driving, and dealing with obnoxious clerks, all while keeping an eye on you to try to make sure that you don't overtax yourself and being ready to help if you do overdo it. That's a lot of work! So be patient with her, let her do things her way even if you'd do things differently, and encourage her to do a few things that you can't do or aren't interested in. Just because you're exhausted and want to go to bed at 8pm doesn't mean your buddy has to stay in the hotel room with you, even if she's your spouse. Instead of making her stay with you when you're taking a long afternoon nap, send her out to take a hike or see a show.

Most importantly—do everything you can to keep yourself as healthy and flare-free as possible. If you're watching out for yourself, she won't have as much work or as much stress, and she'll be able to enjoy her trip much more.

Another great way to say "thank you" to your travel buddy for all their help is to pay for all or part of their travel expenses. This arrangement can be great for both parties—you, because you've got someone who can help you out while you're on the road. And your companion, who might not have the financial resources to travel on her own. This isn't "charity" either—you're asking your companion to take on important tasks and responsibilities. Yes, this does mean that you may need to budget for an additional person when you plan your trips. That's one of the real and unavoidable down sides of traveling with pain. But then again, a car-based trip can be arranged to cost little more for two people than it does for one. Research thoroughly, think creatively, and plan well in advance, and you might be surprised at how little your traveling companion's expenses end up costing you.

Other options include group trips, package tours, and cruises. These options are especially good if you're planning a trip overseas. As always, you've got to let the tour operator know in advance that you've got a medical condition and may need special assistance and someone to keep a lookout for you. The good news is that they'll do it. And not only will there be aware and informed staff members who can help you, your fellow group members may be able to spare a few moments and lend a hand as well. For chronic pain patients who've not spent a lot of time away from home, a package tour can be a way to meet new people, make new friends, and even find some potential travel buddies with similar interests and budgets for future trips.

Any number of tour operators and guide companies specifically work with travelers with disabilities. Most of these tend to cater more towards folks with limited mobility, but they're equipped for a variety of special and unusual needs. I-Can-Travel.com, a resource site for disabled travelers, has lists of links to international accessible tour operators.

Chapter 2: Packing and Preparing

Packing is key to any great vacation, no matter what your health status. When you're traveling with chronic pain, packing right can make the difference between a wonderful trip and a not-so-wonderful trip.

Pack light and smart. Hefting too many heavy bags filled with excess clothing can cause a flare-up, but forgetting a bottle of pills can be devastating. It's a great idea to make a list of must-have items (many of which are described in the next sections), then check off items as you put them into your bags.

A Big List of Numbers

Maybe the most important thing to pack for any trip of any length is a list of important phone numbers. Many of these numbers won't be the same as the friends you call daily on your cell phone. But your cell phone contact list can make a great place to store these numbers. So can a piece of paper stashed in your luggage just in case something happens to your cell phone.

Key Numbers:

- Primary Care Physician
- Specialists and Other Doctors (those who manage your chronic conditions, prescribe your medications, and that you see regularly)
- Hospital or Clinic On-Call (24-hour)
- Home Pharmacy
- Medical Insurance Carrier (be sure to include international-access phone numbers if you're traveling abroad)

- Car Insurance Carrier (if you're renting a car)
- Auto Club (if you or a travel companion will be traveling by car)
- Rental Car Agency (if applicable)
- Hotel/Inn Front Desk Phone (for each hotel)
- Taxi Service (for each destination)
- Airline Passenger Service (or rail carrier, or bus carrier)
- Home and Pet Sitters

Tip: Create one phone list for each bag you're packing. That way if a bag goes astray or is inaccessible, you'll still have all your important numbers.

Medications

It might seem more convenient to leave all the prescription bottles at home and just carry enough meds to get you through your trip. But what happens if weather causes a flight delay, and you're away from home for an extra day? What if you need more pain meds than you anticipated? What if a security or customs agent chooses to challenge your need for a controlled substance you've been legally prescribed?

Pack all the pill bottles, even though it seems like a pain in the patootie. Keep the bottles with you even if you usually use a daily pill-dispenser. The bottles have the prescription numbers, the name of your doctor, and the phone number of your home pharmacy on them. That's some good information, which will satisfy most security and customs agents. That information can also help your traveling companion or even an out-of-town doctor help you in an emergency.

It's also a good idea to carry copies of your written prescriptions with you when you're on the road—especially if you're traveling abroad. Not all the same prescription drugs are available in every country of the world. But if you've got copies of your scripts, a foreign doctor can work with you to find a reasonable replacement for any medication you need.

Pack all your medication in your carry-on luggage for any air travel.

Tip: The TSA must allow more than 3 ounces of liquid or gel for medical use. If you take liquid medications, see the TSA's guidelines for packing and carrying medical liquids and gels.

Medical Devices and Implants

If you have a medical implant, wear prosthesis, or use any assistive devices, be prepared to explain your device and to be scrutinized by airport security. You may be forced to remove exterior prosthetics for screening. Know the TSA regulations about medical devices, and advocate for yourself early and often. Keep a copy of documentation explaining your device and its (and your) needs with you, and furnish it to security agents as needed.

Airplane security rules are a moving target. For the latest TSA rules, regulations, and restrictions on medical devices, check these two web pages:

http://www.tsa.gov/travelers/airtravel/specialneeds/editorial_1374.shtm
http://www.tsa.gov/travelers/airtravel/specialneeds/editorial_1370.shtm

It can be challenging to drag supplemental oxygen tanks onto a plane. Some newer oxygen concentrator devices are FAA approved for commercial air travel, though they can be heavy and have limited battery life. Absolutely inform the airline in advance if you plan to travel with a concentrator, so that you can get a seat near an electrical outlet and get the assistance you need with situating yourself and the machine when you board the plane.

Food and nutrition supplements can be bulky and heavy. Be sure to allow enough room in your bags for all the nutrients you'll need. To minimize weight and bulk, remove supplements from their packages and pack them into Ziploc bags. Be careful with pills to keep them from getting crushed.

Shoes and Clothes (In That Order)

One pair of comfortable walking shoes can get you through a two-week trip like nothing else can. Shoes get heavy and bulky to pack, so try to get by on no more than 2-3 pairs, total. A good rule of footwear:

- One pair of go-everywhere shoes
- One pair of dress shoes for evenings out
- One pair of specialty footwear, if absolutely necessary (sandals for warm climates, boots for snow or for hiking)

Now that you've planned out which shoes you're taking, choose clothes that will match those shoes. This might seem like a backwards way of planning outfits, but it's actually easier to pick mix-and-match outfits and to control the amount of clothing you pack by creating a shoe-based trip wardrobe.

Pack fewer articles of clothing than you think you'll need. Except for underwear. For a 1-2 week trip, one fancy going-out-evenings outfit should suffice. (Don't worry—no one will think less of you for wearing the same dress or shirt twice!) Same for the swimsuit and the snowsuit, though more than one business suit may be required if you're on a weeks-long business trip.

While traveling, you'll be walking more, sitting in lots of uncomfortable chairs, standing lots, possibly eating out in fancier restaurants than usual. If you're traveling abroad or to other parts of the country, the standard of dress may be more formal or more casual than you're accustomed to at home. The weather may be different from anything you've experienced. For example, on Maui it's about 75 degrees and humid every single day of the year. There's no point in bringing a wool sweater.

Go heavy on comfort and short on style if you must make choices, but don't completely discount the fashion sense of locals at your destination. In Paris, visitors get better service in restaurants when they wear slacks and jackets rather than jeans and t-shirts.

Medical Evacuation Insurance, Trip Insurance: Yes or No?

Trip insurance can reimburse you the costs of travel, lodgings, and other prepaid vacation expenses in specific cases. Before purchasing trip insurance, read the fine print! You might not get reimbursed if you cancel your trip yourself for health (or other) reasons.

Medical evacuation insurance is meant for adventurous travelers who climb mountains, trek into the wilderness, and venture to distant lands. If you are injured or fall ill while climbing to the top of Mt. Kilimanjaro, a medical evacuation insurance provider will pay for a helicopter to pull you off the mountain. They'll then fly you out to whatever hospital you choose, around the world.

What medical evac insurance won't do is substitute for or supplement regular medical insurance, either in your home country or abroad. For supplemental insurance, talk with your current insurance carrier. Leave the medical evacuation insurance for your major adventure travel only.

Before you plan that fabulous trip abroad, take a good long look at your medical insurance plan. Does it cover medical treatment overseas? How about prescriptions? Are there any restrictions on international medical coverage? You might be able to find this information online, but sometimes such information is not so readily available. Expect to spend some time on the phone wading through the customer service phone system.

Not all United States HMOs cover international medical treatment. Medicare does not cover any international medical expenses. If your insurance company doesn't cover you when you're abroad, you'll need to purchase supplemental travel medical insurance for the duration of your trip.

The State Department website covers all the basics for international travelers working out their medical insurance needs at http://travel.state.gov/travel/cis_pa_tw/cis/cis_1470.html. This page lists U.S.-based and foreign medical evacuation companies, and of the major reputable travel medical insurance providers. These lists may not be up-to-date—always do your own research to vet any insurance company you purchase a policy from. Know that neither this book nor the State Department endorse any of these companies. A check with the Better Business Bureau at the time this book was written shows that Mondial Assistance (formerly Access America), Seven Corners, and Insuremytrip.com all have 'A' ratings and are accredited by the BBB.

Chapter 3: Getting There

On the Road Again: Driving to Distant Destinations

An American classic, the solo-vehicle road trip can be a versatile way to travel with pain. But it's got its pitfalls, so be sure to prepare carefully before you hop behind the wheel for a cross-country adventure.

Sitting jammed into one position for hours on end hurts. But several things can help mitigate the stiff joints and other aches of long rides. First, pack the car for optimal comfort. Don't jam the back seat so full that you're forced to keep the back of the front seats upright. Keep the back clear so you can pop the seat back down as far as it will go. Obviously, you're not going to drive like that! But even in the driver's seat, you can jimmy your seat position over the hours, thus jimmying your own position and keeping your pain moderated.

Second, plan frequent stops—much more frequent than a healthy road-tripper might take. If you need to stop every single hour to get out and stretch, do it! After all, this is your trip—you can take all the time you want. You'll need a patient traveling companion, of course. I find that small-bladdered folks make ideal road-trip buddies, because they need to stop often too.

Third, take small daily travel bites. If that means your body can only tolerate four hours in a car, or three, or two—then drive for that long, then stop for the night. Again—your trip, your body, your pain, YOUR RULES! No one's giving out prizes for the longest and most torturous time spent in a car, so don't try to win one.

Unless you're driving a SmartCar, you've got at least a little bit of space in your ride for creature comforts, so use it. Load the car with your favorite travel pillows, fuzzy socks, battery-powered heating pads, cooling packs, iPods filled with soothing music, snacks, drinks…anything you can think of that will make your trip more comfortable. I'm particularly fond of my lumbar support pillow and my u-shaped neck pillow, and my super-fuzzy socks. When I'm not driving, I always take off my shoes and get as comfy as possible.

Obviously you'll also want a GPS device or maps. (I like to have a map as backup to my GPS, which has steered me wrong more than once.) And anyone, regardless of their health status, should have an emergency kit with basic first aid supplies in their car on a road trip. Think flares, flashlight, band-aids, gauze, and any other supplies you need for your specific health needs. I pack painkillers and that additional supply of all prescription meds that I keep harping on.

Riding the Rails: Train Travel

I adore traveling by train. It's such an elegant way to get from A to B. In the United States it's doable, in Europe it's essential, and in other parts of the world it's best to check on reliability before climbing aboard.

These days, with comfort often more important than speed, train travel has more appeal than ever. The worst seats on the average (non-commuter) train are similar to the best seats on the average 737-700.

Not all train accommodations are created equal. These days, you must reserve a seat in advance on most trains, even if it's only a few minutes in advance. For travelers with pain, this is a good thing. A reservation means a guaranteed seat of a certain type. In the States, Coach Class means an airline-style bucket seat that's mercifully larger than an economy seat on a plane. Commuter routes often have a Business Class, which means a bigger bucket seat and free non-alcoholic beverages in the club car. First class means a whopping big bucket seat with at-seat food and beverage service on commuter trains. On cross-country routes, Roomettes and Bedrooms offer private compartments with bunks that can be made up into real beds, letting travelers lie down and doze during the day, and get at least some chance of a decent night's sleep on overnight journeys. Those beds can mean the difference between agony and ecstasy if you've got to travel while you're in bad shape, whether you'll be on board the train overnight or not. The top tier bedrooms even have miniscule private bathrooms. Roomettes have no bathroom and don't have cushy chairs in addition to the bunks.

First Class also means first crack at the full hot meals served in the dining car—what's less commonly known is that on many long-haul Amtrak trains, the First Class passengers are occasionally the only passengers who get to eat in the dining car. Sometimes there's simply not enough time, room, or food on board to serve the coach passengers. If you're traveling in Coach on Amtrak, plan to either bring your own food or to purchase snacks such as microwaveable ramen or hot dogs in the club car.

Coach passengers often need to negotiate jostling aisles and shaking narrow stairways to get to the bathroom and the club car concessionary. To avoid dealing with at least some of the stairs, identify yourself as disabled when you purchase your ticket. You'll be granted a seat in a special section, usually right near the restrooms and in bigger seats than the standard economy class. One of the staff is assigned to help you when you need it—including purchasing your food and drink if you can't walk the length of the train to the club car. Whatever class of seat or room you're in; walking from one car to another can be a tough trip. The slowish American trains rock and roll from sea to shining sea. Use handholds, and only get up and walk when you really need to.

The cost of train travel is intensely reasonable if you can tolerate a trip in Coach, and violently expensive if you prefer to go First Class. Coach seats run $75-$200 for most trips, even long routes. Business class and roomettes cost about four times what a Coach seat would—figure about $400-$600. First Class seats cost in the $500-$700 range, while First Class bedrooms can cost up to $1,500 for round-trip. Ouch! The price of comfort can really rip the guts out of the average wallet.

Don't think you'll be able to sneak from your coach seat into an empty First Class bedroom to catch a few horizontal zzzs. The car attendants constantly keep watch for just that, and actively keep all but legitimate passengers out of the First Class cars.

Hair of the Dog: Taking the Bus

I avoid bus travel like the smelly plague it is. But I've got the advantage of having a bunch of generous (and flexibly employed) friends who will drive me most anywhere I can get to by road. If that weren't the case, I'd probably spend a lot more time enjoying the comforts and bemoaning the inconveniences of bus travel.

Bus seats can be reasonably comfortable—big and sometimes reclinable, but please don't take my word as gospel. Seat styles vary by bus line and by bus, in fact. For the most plush comfort and amenities, high end charter buses can't be beat—some such buses even have seat-back digital TV screens these days. The newest and shiniest of the Greyhounds have Wi-Fi and electrical outlets at every seat. The ride tends to be smoother on a bus than on an American train. The variety of routes and destination far outpaces that of the Amtrak system, especially out in the West.

Greyhound, along with most charter companies, offers reasonable assistance for disabled passengers. That assistance gets better the more notice the disabled passenger provides the bus company about her needs. The driver can help you board and assist you with your luggage.

On the down side, bus trips tend to be lengthy and are subject to the traffic whims of their urban destinations. Aside from the seat, there's little room for a passenger to spread out, and only the tiny aisle to walk in. Rest stops happen regularly, but not always in the best of neighborhoods—it's not always advisable to go for a quick walk. Come to think of it, the bus stations you must embark and disembark from don't always perch on the best streets in town either. If you're traveling alone and must switch buses, check out the locations of the bus stations in advance and keep the neighborhoods in mind.

No food is sold or provided on typical bus routes, though some charter trips may offer meals as part of the excursion. On long hauls, you can bring your own food (by far the best option), buy fast food or junk food during the rest stops, or starve.

Of course, the bus is cheap. A Greyhound bus trip from New York City to Washington D.C. costs $40-$70. Greyhound also offers a boon for travelers with disabilities who travel with a companion and who notify the company in advance—a half-price ticket for your companion.

Long-haul buses (Greyhound and charter tour buses) have in-transit bathrooms. Yeah, I know. Bus bathrooms—ick. But still, better than nothing when you've really got to go. That can actually make a bus ride more comfortable than a car trip. Bring your own toilet paper, just to be safe.

Cruisin': All Boats Great and Small

Stereotypes claim that a cruise is a great way to travel for the older, less mobile crowd. I'm always skeptical of those kinds of claims. Cruise ships keep on getting bigger. How many stairs are there? How much walking to get from the dining room to the swimming pool to the staterooms? And how small and uncomfortable are those famously tiny staterooms, really? So, with a need to write about cruises for Traveling with Pain the book, I cautiously embarked on a 3-day Carnival cruise from Long Beach to Ensenada. ('Cause it was cheap and in California.)

I stand convinced. In fact, I sit on a comfy sofa convinced– big cruise ships really do have what's needed to make travel with pain or disability not just possible but comfortable and fun. The biggest trick: let the cruise company know in advance what you need. If they know how to accommodate you, they'll do it.
Staterooms

Typical interior and window staterooms are small but not as miniscule. Two adults can comfortably share a room, stowing their bags so that they can walk around their beds without tripping over each other or their things. Beds are often a point of pride for cruise ships, with comfortable mattresses and high thread count sheets. Bathrooms, while small, aren't any tinier than a typical European hotel bath. Expect to get a stall shower if you're in an economy room on an inexpensive cruise line; bathtubs tend to be reserved for folks who can afford suites. Speaking of suites—they're really nice if you can afford 2-4 times the cost of a standard stateroom to get more space with big squishy sofas, a balcony, and a Jacuzzi tub. Suite patrons get special attentions from the service staff as well.

But if you've got special needs, and you mention them to the cruise line in advance, you can get extra service and help too, for no additional cost.

Fun facts to know and share—the wheelchair accessible staterooms aren't any bigger than the regular ones. The differences are that the tripping steps up into the bathroom have ramps attached, the showers have benches and hand rails, and the desks and safes are set lower for easier access.

Navigating the Ship

Strolling around a large cruise ship is pleasantly simple. Banks of elevators crawl up and down the decks at regular intervals. Hallways are wide enough for mobility aids. Best of all, most big ships' decks burst with lounges, restaurants, bars, and buffets, all with seats anyone can plop down in at any time. High-traffic areas offer comfy sofas and seating specially placed so that strollers can stop and sit a while any time they want to—wonderful for travelers with pain who can't always walk long distances without resting.

On-Board Activities

Many of the activities printed so cutely on the ship's daily newsletter involved lots of sitting and little heavy exercise. Watching the Hairy Chest Contest on the Lido Deck didn't cause me too much physical strain, though emotionally I may be scarred forever.

The deck chairs were regrettably hard when I lounged outside with my romance novel, but I think they're supposed to be like that.

Shore Excursions

Also easy and comfy are many of the trips ashore. Read the tour descriptions carefully and you'll find the wheelchair accessible ones–those will be the easiest, requiring the least walking and no climbing or other strenuousness.

Air Travel: Extra Sarcasm Not Necessary

I could write a whole book about decreasing the pain of plane rides. But the most important thing to understand is simple: air travel is exhausting and painful. Even healthy people stumble off planes nursing muscle spasms and whimpering with fatigue. Expect the pain, expect the fatigue, and you'll do better at mitigating both.

Start thinking about your (relative) comfort during your travel when you're booking your flights. If you'll be enduring connections, make sure that you've got at least an hour between each flight. Whether you're sure you'll need it or not, check the box requesting wheelchair assistance at the airport. There's no penalty if you're able to walk the airport on the day of the flight.

I strongly recommend packing a bag to check, and the lightest carry-on possible. Of course medications and prescription and doctor info must go in the carry-on. But clothes, toiletries, shoes, extra books…let the baggage handlers carry these things. Yes, to check a bag is to take a risk that it will be lost. For me, it's worth that risk to literally lighten my load. Your experiences may vary.

The most comfortable and pleasant flight you can manage starts even before you even get into the car to go to the airport. These few things will make the whole experience better:

• Relax

Soothe your muscles as much as possible. Take a long hot bath or shower. Get a massage if you can afford to, or ask a friend for a shoulder rub. Put ice or a heating pad on your most painful points an hour or two before you leave for the airport.

- Eat

Eat a full meal including protein an hour or so before you leave for the airport. For the pleasure of it, indulge in a few bites of dessert too. Then pack an easy-to-eat meal for the plane–again, making sure there's protein included.

- Dress

Put on your most comfortable clothes (yay yoga pants!), planning for an air-conditioned terminal and plane. Keep your final destination in mind. Wear layers you can peel off if you're headed someplace warm and humid, or carry a warm coat if your destination will be chilly.

I pack my carry-on bag as lightly as possible. It never ends up being as light as I want it to be, but I try. Here are a few useful and stress-reducing things to pack (or recommend packing) into your carry-on:

- Meds

All of them, in their individual prescription bottles, always, without exception.

- Copies of prescriptions, with doctor signatures

If something happens to your prescription bottles, copies of prescriptions could save you. You can bring them to a local doctor or hospital and request duplicate prescriptions if a bottle was lost or stolen.

Copies of prescriptions can be especially useful and important if you're traveling abroad for an extended period of time.

- Letters from doctors

Anyone who's got a medical implant, a prosthetic limb, or any other medical device should carry a letter from a physician to present to airport security at the TSA checkpoints. The more documentation you carry, the less likely it is that you'll have trouble being cleared through security screening to your gate in an almost timely fashion.

If you have any unusual treatment needs, or it's likely that you'll become incapacitated to the point where you can't make medical decisions for yourself, a letter from your doctor might help clarify your condition and requirements in an emergency.

If it's likely that you'll need local medical help at your destination, get a letter from your doctor describing your condition and treatment plan. Include phone numbers, including pager or on-call physician numbers at your usual hospital if you believe an untimely emergency could occur.

- Pillows

I have a bead-filled half-circle neck pillow that I cherish and bring on all my longer flights despite its inconvenient size and shape. Inflatable neck pillows take up far less space and may be more convenient for you. Because so many planes no longer supply any kind of pillow or blanket, you may also want to bring a small inflatable pillow to bolster your lower back.

- Heat or cold packs

No gel packs of any temperature over 3 oz, of course. For cold, I recommend going old school. That is, bring an empty zip-locking bag and a towel. Ask the flight attendants for ice. Put ice in bag and wrap bag in towel. Apply ice bag to achy joint.

For heat, I shop at camping or motorcycle stores for small but powerful hot packs. Bikers put these in their gloves and boots to keep their extremities from going numb on cold rides. They work best *outside* of a layer or two of clothing.

- Food

Yes, you are allowed to bring your own food onto airplanes. I do it for just about every flight I take that's more than an hour long.

Protein is key. I like nuts and hardboiled eggs. Veggies, like carrot and celery sticks, with humus or nut butter work well. On longer flights, I'll put together a complex salad in a plastic container, with a couple of ounces of vinaigrette dressing in a separate container.

I also usually pack myself a cookie or a brownie—some sort of satisfying sweet that helps me to feel full. And for a cheaper way to keep hydrated, I bring an empty steel water bottle through security then fill it up for the wait at the gate.

- Lightweight entertainment and distraction

I love my paperback novels. My boyfriend prefers his PSP. iPads and netbooks and Kindles weigh mere ounces and contain multiple days' worth of entertainment. Kids can be calmed by their favorite videos on a compact DVD player.

Don't expect a personal seat-back on entertainment unit on every flight, especially on older bargain airlines like Alaska and Southwest. Always be prepared to provide your own distraction both at the airport and in the air.

- Earplugs and sleep masks

Sensory deprivation is key for me to be able to sleep on a longer flight, and I prefer a specific style of earplug. (Transatlantic carriers usually provide cheap disposable masks and earplugs.) And there's a rumor that sleeping promotes health and well-being.

- Slip-on shoes

If you possibly can, wear slip-on shoes to the airport. The more complicated the shoes, the harder it's going to be to wrestle them off, then tie/buckle/zip/weld them back on after the security scan.

The next step to a pain-minimal trip is to approach the airport with a plan. Good terminal rituals minimize discomfort, stress, and trouble before you board.

- Arrive early

Plan to be at the airport an hour and a half before your takeoff time for domestic (US, EU) flights and two and a half to three hours for international flights. Even skycap lines can get horrifically long on popular flight days and times. Expect to have to wait in several lines, to wait up to 30 minutes for wheelchair service, and to be picked out for special searching at Security. If none of this happens, you'll just spend a bit of extra time sitting at the gate waiting to board your plane.

Better bored than panicked.

- Get the wheelchair

I don't think I can emphasize this one point enough—even if you don't feel like you "deserve" wheelchair service from the terminal to the gate, or it embarrasses you, or whatever…ask for the wheelchair anyhow. It will take miles off your journey. (Possibly in a literal sense, depending on the length of the security lines!)

Wheelchair service at airports exists because the airlines and airports know how hard it is to get from one end of a modern airport to the other. They know that the folks who request wheelchairs at the airport may not need mobility assistance everywhere they go. You, as someone who's got any problem that might make it hard and painful to get from the ticket counter to the jet way, are exactly the person they had in mind. So request the wheelchair if there's any chance at all that you might need it or want it, just to make your trip a little bit easier.

- Go to the bathroom

Take advantage of the bigger and more comfortable facilities in the airport before you board the plane. Wait as long as possible and hit the restroom right before pre-boarding begins.

- Be nice to airport staff (even if they're not nice to you)

When I start to sink into a "boy my life sucks" funk, I take a moment to try to imagine what it must be like to work in a busy airport. Imagine getting to tell already stressed and unhappy people that their flights are overbooked, delayed, or cancelled every day—then rebook them onto other flights.

So smile at airport staff, and try not to get snappish even when things go wrong. It's a pretty safe bet that the gate agent didn't go out and break the airplane toilets herself, just to delay your flight. And she certainly doesn't control the weather, so the fog that just closed the whole airport really isn't her fault.

- Avoid the bar

The drinks are overpriced, watered down, and a bad idea when combined with most medications. Just don't go there.

- Keep a tight leash on carry-ons

It's not a chronic pain thing; it's a chronic traveler thing. Hook the straps of your bags around your wrists and ankles, and keep zippers closed. Even when you're reading, devote a bit of attention to keeping an eye on your things.

- Stretch and breathe

Especially if you're waiting out a delay or an early arrival, do some in-chair stretches and stand up to stretch out your back and pump some blood into your legs every 15-30 minutes.

While airports might be a great place for full-fledged mediation, some deep breathing exercises reduce physical stress and relieve emotional tension.

Finally, you've made it through check-in and security, to the gate, up the ramp, and into my assigned seat. Hooray! Now you've only got 2 (4, 6, 10, 12…) hours of sitting there in a metal tube hurtling through the sky towards your destination.

Here are my favorite coping strategies for the long, boring, cramped part of the journey:

- Ask for/accept help stowing your carry-on

If you've got a heavy bag that needs to be slung up into the overhead bin, ask for help. Flight attendants are almost always willing to do this, and even other passengers can be shockingly helpful and friendly. Not straining your back and shoulders right before stuffing them into an airplane seat makes the whole flight feel less awful.

The one problem with overhead bins? It's a big pain to open them in-flight to get anything out of a bag. Try to avoid putting anything up there that you might need (like meds) while you're still on the plane.

These days, I stow both my carry-on and my purse under the seat in front of me. (Yeah, I keep 'em that small.) That way I've got my meds, my book, my food, and my cell phone all sitting right there where I can access them easily. Anything I don't absolutely need to use in-flight I put into my checked bag. I find this so, so much easier than trying to deal with a gigantic carry-on. Also, I'm amassing good travel karma because I'm not taking up precious (and almost always overflowing) overhead bin space.

- Eat and drink regularly on long flights

On long flights, try to keep the same eating schedule you use at home. For me, that's eating every 4 hours. I bring my own food whenever possible because airline food makes me queasy. Try to get something to drink every hour or so.

- Think before drinking

Caffeinated beverages and alcohol aren't the best hydrators ever, though they taste good. They're diuretics–uncomfortable when long lines form for overworked plane latrines. The effects of alcohol (and prescription medications!) are exacerbated by high altitudes. Whee! Might sound like fun, but it gets rapidly less fun as the buzz wears off and baggage claim looms.

• Stretch and walk

Always with the stretching, yes. The easiest things to stretch are neck, shoulders, and wrists–you can do those in your seat. When you get up to walk, you can do a few back looseners, and if you're lucky maybe stretches a quick hamstring. The walking gets more important the longer the flight. On any flight longer than 3 hours, be sure to get up and walk every hour—not only does this help to keep your pain down, it decreases the risk of blood clots forming in your legs. This can be a big, big deal if you've had any recent surgery or major medical procedure.

• Breathe and meditate

In times of flight-induced stress, especially as the hours stretch out on a long flight, your only real respite from the noise and the smells and the pain is to close your eyes and breathe deeply. In flight actually makes for a good place to practice meditation. You're sitting in one spot, without any work you need to do, so why not use the time to quiet your mind and maybe even help your health a tiny bit?

• Sleep (on long flights)

On flights over 3 hours, try to sleep for a while. After a meal and a drink, put in the earplugs, don your sleep mask, recline your seat, and have at it. If it's a super-long flight (10 hours or more), you might even take a sleeping pill—if you don't have a prescription, melatonin supplements may be a good choice-to ensure that you go out for a few hours at least.

• Use the restroom whenever it's free

At the instant the Fasten Seat Belt sign dings off the first time, eject yourself from that seat as though it were on fire. If you're lucky, you'll make it to the bathroom first–no lines for you! Also, you probably won't have to go again right after beverage or meal service, when the rest of the passengers usually go. Watch the "occupied/unoccupied" signs on longer flights, and even if it's not an emergency, get up to use an unoccupied lavatory. If nothing else, it gets you up out of your seat for an hourly walk.

• Smile at the flight attendants

Flight attendant is another job that sounds hard to me. It costs nothing to smile at these folks. Because I sometimes need extra help, it can be useful to have "friends" who are working on the plane.

The plane has landed. It's time to disembark, claim the bags, and hit the hotel. Hoorah! But the stress of this final push can bring on a pain spike if you don't do it right. Here's how I manage that last bit of the trip to create the right start (or finish) for my vacation:

• When the plane lands, chill out.

It is absolutely unnecessary to launch myself out of the plane's door as though propelled by a rocket. Instead, consider letting everyone else push and shove and be first out of the plane. As the aisle empties, amble on out and find your wheelchair.

- Let someone else heave the luggage around.

As much as possible, let the wheelchair attendant or your travel companion deal with the heavier checked bags. The attendants usually do this as part of their chair service. Your travel buddy can also deal with the bags easily enough. Learn to let them. The bag is invariably lighter, easier to roll, and less freak-out inducing than you will be if you overdo it and wind up curled up on the ground moaning in agony.

- Eat.

Because the next step is to sleep for a long while, the first order of business on the ground must be to feed yourself. Try to get something reasonably healthy, with some lean protein. If you get a salad, make sure it's got a boiled egg or grilled chicken or something on it.

- Drop bags, dim lights, insert self into bed, sleep until done.

Don't unpack. Don't explore. Don't go on a quick excursion. Go to **bed**.

Flying is a hard thing to put a body through–altitude changes, dry recycled air, crushingly bad physical positioning, time changes, and stress at every turn… Even when you do everything right before and during the flight, your body will crave rest immediately afterward and this is one time when it's best to give in to the craving.

In my case, I sometimes lose as much as 24 hours at the beginning of my trip to sleeping. But when I wake up from my post-flight mini-hibernation, I'm generally time-adjusted, rested, and ready to get on with the fun!

Chapter 4: Sleeping and Eating

Resting Your Weary Head: Accommodations

If I could just stay at the Four Seasons or the Fairmont every time I leave home, my chronic pain would probably slink off quietly. Seriously—if you've got the money to stay at a four-star resort/spa hotel when you're out and about, do it all you can. The beds are soft and comfortable, the pillows fluffy, the bathtubs deep, and the staff accommodating of all sorts of unusual needs. Luxury hotels are accustomed to quirks far more difficult to deal with than a ground floor room in a quiet part of the property with a scent-free pillow. They tend to have valet parking, golf carts to help mobility-challenged guests move about, and on-site spas with a wealth of services that can relax and de-pain deep-pocked clients.

Aaaand…back to reality.

Because most travelers with pain can't afford ultra-luxe accommodations for every trip, it's a good idea to know what you need and how to get it, within the scope of your travel budget.

What do you need in a bedroom to rest comfortably? Here are a few things to think about:

- Mattress: Do you need soft? Firm? Specialty (like Sleep Number or memory foam)?
- Bedding: Are you allergic to scented detergents or down comforters? Do you need extra blankets to sleep comfortably?
- Pillows: Do you need more than one or two? Can you tolerate down or do you need foam? Do you usually require a body pillow or a knee pillow?
- Room space: Do you require a fair amount of space to move about comfortably with any mobility aids you use?

- Air: Are you scent-sensitive? Temperature sensitive? Accustomed to air conditioning while you sleep?
- Sound: Do you need it quiet when you sleep? Can you tolerate earplugs?
- Light: Do you need it to be full dark to get to sleep? Or do you require some light, a TV, or some other light in your bedroom?
- Bathroom: Do you have any special needs or wants for your bath-away-from-home? A tub? Roll-in or step-in shower? Hand rails? A shower stool? A Jacuzzi?

Unless you actually can afford the Ritz, you probably won't get your ideal hotel room. Once you've gotten your list together, read it back over and make notes on what you can compromise on. You can probably bring your bed pillow from home and maybe a favorite blanket too. Ear plugs can solve many a sound problem (and I so, so highly recommend getting used to earplugs if you plan to travel often). You can bring your own folding stool for the shower, along with your favorite scent-free toiletries if you're allergic to perfumes. But if you're highly scent-sensitive, an inn that drowns its rooms in sweet perfumes won't be a good choice. When traveling, dealing with uncomfortable beds is part of the deal, but if sleep is impossible on concrete-slab like surfaces, the average Motel 6 will probably put you in traction.

So now you've got a list of "must haves" and "high wants" to guide your research. What I do is first check the Internet, to find a few places at my destination that will meet my musts. Orbitz, hotels.com, and TripAvisor are some of my favorites. Friends' recommendations are even better, when I can get them. There's nothing like the word of somebody I trust that's actually slept on the beds, smelled the sheets, and used the commode.

Then, with two or three lodgings in mind, I pick up the phone. Talking to real human beings works so much better for booking a room. These days, not only can you get the accommodations you need at your accommodations, you can often negotiate the price of the room while you're at it. With the travel industry still struggling, a sympathetic desk clerk might be able to shave 10-20 percent off the price of a comfortable room at a good motel or even a bed &

breakfast. I start with my favorite-looking place, and keep calling until I find the right home away from home.

Chain Motels

It's true—most American chain motels aren't terribly enlivening in their décor or ambiance. But what chain motels are is reliable. Whether you're in Oregon, Ohio, New Hampshire, or New Mexico, a Holiday Inn is still a Holiday Inn. The mattresses will be mediocre, the sheets clean, the wall art bland, and the prices moderate. Whereas in the average Motel 6, the mattresses will be rock hard, the sheets questionable, the carpets scary, and the prices rock-bottom. Whereas, at the top of the chain (ha ha) of lodgings, the average Four Seasons hotel offers cloudlike beds boasting linens so white they're almost blinding, luxurious bathrooms, room service, and a staff that really *really* wants to make your stay more comfortable.

When I want information about a specific chain motel, or a chain I'm not familiar with, I go to the AAA hotel guides. Their ratings are concise and not precisely tuned for a traveler with pain, but they're reliable for information about cleanliness, service, and available features like swimming pools, hot tubs, in-room Jacuzzis, and room service.

Inns, Lodges, and Other Independents

Going for the cute little country B&B or the off-the-beaten-path can be the best move you make on your trip, or the worst mistake of your year. Many travelers pick only independent lodgings specifically to avoid the routine predictability of chain motels. But when you're traveling with pain, that fun unpredictability can mean misery, discomfort, sleepless nights, and a wrecked trip.

Bed and breakfast inns can be great for a traveler with pain. They can also be torture. Most B&Bs in the US don't have elevators, so hauling self and stuff up stairs is a frequent occurrence. Beds can range from genuine antique mattresses (complete with original rusted-solid springs!) to brand-new Sleep Numbers or Tempurpedics. And in B&Bs, which specific room you pick can mean the difference between plush ground-floor ease and three flights to the former servant's quarters in the attic. When you call to make reservations, ask about the rooms. Even if you've done your online homework and know which rooms in your chosen inn you want, ask about the mattresses, stairs, noise levels, and bath amenities.

As a traveler with pain, I absolutely positively require real reviews of independent inns before I make a reservation. Again, the AAA guides can help sometimes, though they're not great for truly "off the beaten track" establishments. I've come to like TripAdvisor.com—the user reviews have rarely steered me wrong. For travelers whose pain impairs mobility, Candy Harrigan's book There Is Room at the Inn provides tons of great information about accessible lodgings in the United States.

Boutique and Luxury Hotels

Boutique hotel sounds pretentious, and sometimes the reality is kind of ridiculous. But in big cities, boutique hotels can run from the chic-to-the-point-of-silly W chain to comfy small independents, and on down to artsy and uncomfortable 6-story walk-ups. Before you go berserk for boutiques, be sure you know what you're getting into. If the web site or brochure doesn't mention things like elevators, bell service, or parking availability—call and ask.

Got a couple of thousand dollars burning a hole in your bank account? Me neither. But every once in a while, I think it's worth it to scrimp and save to spend some time in a luxury hotel. These days, most luxury hotels belong to major chains like the Four Seasons and the Fairmont, or to corporate hotel groups like Joie de Vivre and Starwood. The hotels without the chain names tend to have a more independent flavor, while the big names pride themselves on certain standard accoutrements on all their properties.

It's hard to go wrong with a luxury hotel—their purpose in the world is to take in (wealthy) stressed-out travelers and pamper them silly. A traveler with pain will find everything from oversized soaking tubs to a choice of different types of pillows to in-room massages. The only problem—the price. At a Four Seasons or Fairmont level hotel, expect to pay $300 per night at a bare minimum, and $500 per night on average. Suites and such can creep all the way to $1000 per night and beyond. But I've got some happy news—the recession has hit the luxury hotel business hard. This means that a willingness to travel during the off-season, plus a personal phone call, can scrape a hundred bucks or more off the per-night tab at many luxury establishments these days.

Serious travel writers sneer at luxury hotels and resorts. But then, most serious travel writers are hale, healthy men whose only real experiences with pain involve hangover headaches and the occasional sprained ankle. As a travel writer and chronic pain survivor, I love luxury hotels above many, many travel experiences. They're just so comfortable and relaxing at every turn. Every time I've stayed in luxurious digs, I've left in less pain than I had going in. So there.

Hostels

For travelers with pain, hostelling is a mixed bag at best. As a working travel writer, what I love most about hostels is the price. At $15-$25 per night for a bed with a mattress indoors, few lodgings can beat hostels for budget traveling.

In addition to gender segregated and co-ed dorm rooms, many hostels offer one or two private or "family" rooms. At $50-$100 per night, that's not much better pricewise than a cheap motel, but they offer more privacy and comfort for me if I'm not feeling well. So I'll choose based on what I know of the motels and hostels in any given area. Some hostels are pits, some are gorgeous. Hidden Villa Hostel in tony Los Altos, California boasts the best of sustainable architecture set on an organic farm and ranch that backs onto the hiking trails of the Santa Cruz Mountains. On the other hand, the Downtown San Francisco hostel sits adjacent to the dirty and dangerous Tenderloin, and seems to bring a lot of that neighborhood inside. Especially the smell.

I might pick a hostel over a comparable motel if I'm feeling sociable. I love chatting up hostel owners, who tend to be passionate about their regions and great sources of information about where to eat, what to see, and how to do it all cheap. They'll know little about how to work around a chronic disability—disabled folks aren't usually a hostel's bread-and-butter clientele. But if I want a companion or four to hang out with, it's easy enough to hook up with fellow travelers for a night out or a night in, cooking in the ubiquitous hostel common kitchen and chatting in the living spaces.

Hostel kitchens build in another big cost savings while traveling—food. I often prefer to cook many of my own meals on the road—it's a great way to sample the best of local farmer's markets and cook-at-home specialties while saving money, and the pinch of fridge space and dash of stove time make that possible.

There's nothing to cap a pain-ridden travel day quite like drunk people staggering loudly into my dorm room in the middle of the night, turning on the lights, talking for a while, then crashing into the bunk above me and proceeding to snore until dawn. And in a $20 hostel dorm bed, this happens. Staying out late drinking and clubbing, then failing to respect the sleep of dorm-mates is part of hostel culture. As the sick one wanting quiet sleep from midnight on, I'm the odd one out, not them. Expecting a bunch of strangers to cater to my medical needs…isn't reasonable and doesn't work.

In a hostel I don't have any control over temperature in my room. I can ask the staff to adjust the thermostat, but that's about it. And it's not like most hostels include fluffy comforters to snuggle beneath. Granted, more hostels offer bedding included with the price these days. (Check that before you arrive, or you could get a nasty surprise!) But I must lug around an extra blanket and my own pillow to guarantee a reasonably comfortable sleep. And if I can't sleep, I can't travel successfully, period.

Hostels don't have private bathrooms, and I hate dealing with hall bathrooms in the middle of the night in a hostel or hotel full of strangers. At best I feel unwarm; at worst, unsafe. Of course there's nothing so comfortable as a bathtub—I'm lucky to find hot enough, clean enough stall showers in almost all hostels. Cheap shower shoes are friends of hostellers the world over.

It's a rare hostel that boasts a working elevator, and if I'm not feeling well I'm not able to slog bags up and down stairs. Urban hostels often have several flights; rural hostels tend toward uneven ground with hills. Even if US accessibility requirements have been ostensibly met, I usually need some extra energy to negotiate lodgings.

Almost always, hostelling means more physical strain than staying in a motel (though less than camping). Stuffing luggage into lockers, climbing stairs, climbing bunk bed ladders, making my own bed, washing dishes, and getting around the property must all be factored in to a hostel stay.

I've been to some repulsive hostels–dirty, smelly, and dangerously located. Sanitation in any given hostel depends on how good the staff is and how much the operators care. It's almost never great, and it can be terrifyingly bad. If you've got serious food allergies, look at the pots and utensils in a hostel kitchen with suspicion—it's anyone's guess as to what's been on them, and how well (or otherwise) cleaned they've been.

Need a comfortable mattress to get a good night's sleep? Good luck with that. Hostel mattresses run from reasonable to wretched. In the private rooms, I see a lot of futons. I find old futon mattresses only a little bit less comfortable to sleep on than linoleum.

Got allergies, scent sensitivities, light or sound issues? Bummer. Chances that you'll convince the 3-7 strangers in your room to conform to your requirements are slim to none. Hostels cater primarily to young, fit, backpackers who like their nightlife. Travelers staying in hostels may drink, smoke, and do drugs in the room or on the property—it's part of hostel culture. This means that it's really a bad idea to advertise that I take narcotic painkillers. I don't talk about them, and I keep them secured day and night.

I can't usually stay in hostels. I've got too many needs that hostels just can't meet, such as guaranteed quiet while I'm sleeping and private bathroom facilities. Your mileage may vary—if you can manage hostels, they are a great way to get out and travel on the cheap. But before you book your hostel beds, think hard about what you really need to be baseline comfortable when you travel. There's more than money at stake; the physical cost of travel can be high for travelers with pain, and staying in a hostel puts me over my budget for pain.

Eating: Fueling Up

I eat better when I'm traveling than I do at home. But that's me. For many travelers, it becomes all too easy to skip a meal or two each day. Don't do that.

The most important thing to do with or about food when you're traveling is to eat on a regular schedule—your eating schedule from home works best to start with. But on travel, you'll probably be more active than you usually are at home. This means you need lots of fuel to keep your body as healthy or at least functional as possible. So plan for regular meals and healthy snacks throughout the day. Don't skip.

Too Much of a Bad Thing

Under-eating might not be the only food challenge you face on the road. The grabbing of a grease-laden, sugary, nearly nutrient-free fast food meal is all too quick and convenient. On road trips, the golden arches and big purple bells that crowd the side of the freeway can seem like the simplest way to make sure you're getting enough calories without sacrificing driving or sightseeing time.

But the *quality* of the calories matters as much as the quantity. An endless parade of cheeseburgers and fast-food burritos washed down with caffeinated sodas will keep you full, but they won't keep you well. Junk food tends to mess with hormone levels, while sodas cause blood sugar spikes and crashes. You'll end up with less energy to enjoy your travel time. At worst, a sudden diet of fast food might even cause a pain flare that ruins or ends your trip altogether.

To avoid the need to eat convenience foods, add time to your trip for real meals. Plan an hour for breakfast, an hour for lunch, and an hour and a half for dinner. When you know in advance that you're taking that much time to eat, the "fast" part of fast food becomes far less tempting.

Road trippers can add a good sized cooler to their luggage. The cooler never needs to leave the trunk of the car, and it can carry everything from ice-cold water to fresh fruit to fancy cheeses. I love having that cooler not just because I can pack it with inexpensive food from my local grocery store before I leave, but then I can also pick up perishable local delicacies that I wouldn't be able to carry without refrigeration.

Instead of burger joints, stop at farm stands and buy fruits and vegetables grown locally in season. Rather than buying packaged sugar-bombs at gas stations, look for grocery stores frequented by locals—the selection's better and the healthier food will be cheaper in the bargain.

Plan plenty of picnics. Seeking out spots to dine outdoors provides not only a place to eat a meal, but often an opportunity to enjoy a park, winery grounds, beach, historic town square…you get the idea. There's no need to confine picnics to lunchtime either—a sunset dinner on top of a mountain or a dawn feast on the beach creates a change of pace that helps make even a trip to the next town over from your home just a little bit more exotic and special.

Set aside at least one evening (or afternoon, or morning) to enjoy a meal in a restaurant. While I love those gourmet goodies piled high on white plates that get served in super-spendy restaurants, it's not necessary to hock your house to get a great meal "out" on travel. If you can't afford haute cuisine, ask around and find the best breakfast diner in town. Or check out regional, seasonal specialty dining—in Apple Hill, California, many orchards serve apple-based fare during harvest season.

Too Much of a Good Thing

Say you do have enough discretionary budget to patronize the very best restaurants your destinations have to offer. After all, culinary tourism has become an immense industry, and everyone from five-star restaurants to rural farm stands seek the business of travelers. Trying the best food your destination has to offer can be an irresistible temptation.

But all that irresistible food can start to weigh you down after a few days, and I'm not referring to a pound or two on the waistline. The real problem is that lots of rich food that's not part of your usual day-to-day diet can affect your immediate physical well-being. So stop and think before picking up your cell phone and making reservations at a different high-end restaurant for every lunch and dinner throughout your vacation. Fancy food tends to be heavy with buttery sauces and shining demi-glace. And despite the small-looking portions on each plate, gourmet meals often include multiple courses that add up to far more calories than diners realize they're consuming. That's not even including the fine wines that often accompany such meals.

Extra calories mean a need for extra energy to digest each meal. Unusual foods can mean unusual food sensitivity reactions, especially in people who have other health problems.

Plus, all that fancy Top Chef-esque food gets really monotonous after a while. Seriously. Mix it up—light meals most of your trip, with one or two top tier dining experiences mixed in.

Chapter 5: Sightseeing

Day at the Museum: Getting your culture on

I love museums. Big ones, tiny ones, specialized museums and generalized houses of culture and art. But enjoying a day of museums can take a lot out of me. Like most parts of traveling with pain, it pays to plan ahead, even if it's only a few hours or a day ahead.

Many large museums, especially (but not exclusively) in the United States have provisions for mobility-challenged patrons. Aisles are wide and galleries large. Often museums will rent wheelchairs for guests who need them only temporarily. If you're having a bad day (or week, or month, or year) take them up on this service. In the Met or the Smithsonian, you'll walk five miles and only cover half the museum's ground! A chair will take the strain off and let you spend as much time as you like enjoying your favorite painting or sculpture or stealth military jet.

Consider calling ahead to ask whether or not your target museum has seating in the galleries. Some museums are much better than others about offering banquettes in the middle of the galleries, or inconspicuous folding chairs along the wall. These seats are meant to be used, so if you're starting to wear out, plop your butt down. You won't look sick or weird—you'll look like an avid art lover who's studying a favorite work in great depth.

Small museums are a hidden gem for travelers with pain. In the States, counties, cities, state parks, hobbyists, and historic sites often create their own little historical or specialty museums. These things often only take up one or two rooms, which make them totally untiring and easy to enjoy for half an hour without any guilt because you've already seen everything. Best of all, you'll be seeing something that every other tourist might not have found.

Little museums also have the advantage of being cheap, sometimes even free. (I beg you—if you go to a free local museum, give as much of a donation as you can. Let's help keep these little gems going!) You won't usually find painful lines or hideous crowds either. That makes small museums a much better choice for folks with allergies and scent sensitivities, as well as for travelers who can't stand idle in line for hours on end.

Do be aware that the little museums usually don't have the money for wide aisles or mobility aids. Be prepared to be mildly inconvenienced that way, or to do a short walk.

The one part of museuming I don't love is special exhibitions at big art museums. Sure, you can see some awesome stuff from places around the world that might be outside of your current travel perimeters. But...ouch. You get to stand in line for tickets or will-call. Then you get to stand in line to get in the door. Then you're herded like a Jersey cow through the exhibits, always surrounded by your fellow exhibitionists and never encouraged to sit down or even stop moving. Exhibition = exhaustion, and exhaustion = pain flare. Honestly, it's not worth it most of the time.

Monuments, Cathedrals, Pyramids, and Mines
A great way to feel accomplished without doing very much

Monuments are a great thing to see when you're traveling with pain. Why? Because you don't usually have to do very much other than stand there and look at them to have a good experience. At places like the Eiffel Tower and the Empire State Building, you can ride the elevator up to the top, and the lines for those rides can be daunting. But a lightweight folding stool can solve the problem of standing in line for half an hour, and the elevator rides themselves aren't strenuous (or long). Once up at the top, most tower-shaped monumental buildings offer benches from which to admire the startling views. (And if not, you've got that stool you used in line.) Snap a few photos, and the next thing you know, you've completed a full fledged travel experience.

Churches and cathedrals are some of my favorite sightseeing destinations. Whatever church you're visiting, even if it's as famed and crowded as the St. Paul in the Vatican or Notre Dame in Paris, you can sit down and rest for as long as you need to. In a church, you can walk, or not, as much as you want to, or can.

Other attractions can be a bigger challenge to travelers with pain. Before buying tickets for that camel-ride out to the Great Pyramid at Giza, or even for the tour of an old mine in California's Gold Country, consider carefully. What kind of effort will it take just to get to this amazing place? And once you've made it to the entrance, how much walking, climbing, and crawling is required to take the tour? Remember that in many cool historical mansions and tombs, there's no backing out of the tour after you've started. If you get all the way up to the top of a fabulous tower in a Scottish castle, but the stairs made your pain spike, you won't find a convenient elevator with a padded seat to take you back down to the ground level. And after you've stooped and bent and folded yourself to get through a series of tunnels and into a fabulous natural limestone cavern, you must do it all again to get back out.

So think hard not just about getting there and reaching your goal location, but about finishing a whole tour and then getting back not just to the entrance of the attraction but all the way back to your lodgings. Can you do it all without flaring your pain? If you don't think you can, how bad do you think the pain will be? If you take painkillers, how will that impact your ability to walk, climb stairs, ride horses, drive cars if needed?

And finally, will seeing this particular place—be it castle or cave, pyramid or mansion—be worth the pain it may cause? For me, that depends on whether I've been to this amazing place before, and whether I'm likely to ever come back to the place. Do I need to risk a serious flare to take yet another tour of Hearst Castle, which I've been to twice and sits an easy distance from my home? No, probably not. On the other hand, I might not make it to Macchu Pichu more than once in my lifetime. So I'd be more willing to take painkillers, stretch lots for the days before the climb and just man up and endure the pain, thus giving myself a chance for a genuine once-in-a-lifetime adventure to see a truly astonishing piece of human history up close.

The choice will always be yours, and it can be a difficult decision to make. As you travel more, you'll learn how to balance your own scales—pain and fatigue on one plate and personal experience on the other—and how to make these choices well.

Zoos and Aquariums
Emus and flamingos and meerkats, oh my!

Kids of all ages love zoos, both aquatic and land-based. And some of them, like the San Diego Zoo and the Monterey Bay Aquarium, have become major attractions for travelers from around the world. Smaller municipal zoos pull mostly local families out for a weekend of semi-wild animals and kid-energy-draining.

If you're headed for one of the major zoos or aquariums, call ahead and ask about accessibility of seating, motorized tour options, and availability of mobility aids. Also ask about the size of the parking lots, distance to the main gates from the parking area, and the usual length of the lines for tickets and admittance.

Advance planners can skip at least one line at many major zoos and aquariums by buying tickets online. Municipal multi-attraction tourist passes often include the local wild animal hangouts, and can be a genuine bargain if you hit more than two of the included places. Lots of these kinds of things can be found on the Internet. Also look at the brochures and tour guide publications in your hotel—they often include both the info you'll need to purchase tickets to the zoo, and a coupon to get those tickets cheaper.

Use all the assistance the big zoos and aquariums offer. Get a map and take a few minutes to study it before you set off on your adventure. Otherwise, it's all to easy to wander from enclosure to enclosure, then realize an hour later that you're lost and exhausted and you've got two more miles to walk if you want to see the meerkats.

The San Diego Zoo is freakin' huge, but you can take a tram tour in a circle around the property to get a glimpse of many of the furred and feathery residents without hiking several hilly miles. And if you find yourself at the top of the hill, the aerial tram ride can get you back down again. The Zoo rents motorized scooters and wheelchairs at the gate, and attendants get free admission, but keep in mind that the push up some of the hills in a standard wheelchair can make for more of a workout for your travel buddy than he or she might want.

To get a longer sit-down break, take in a show. Places like Sea World have planned shows every few hours that will let you sit back and let the dolphins and sea lions do the moving. Zoos often have feeding and training shows, though seating for them can be iffy. Get to the appointed area early and fold out your stool toward the front to enjoy a few minutes of respite while the snake starts swallowing a rat.

Zoos and aquariums are good places to bring small folding stools—otherwise a seat when you start to tire will not be guaranteed. Most zoos are open air affairs, so bring a hat, long sleeved shirt, and sunscreen in the summer, and an umbrella and a slicker in the winter. The good news is that the outdoor nature of the zoo will help disperse any scents your fellow patrons are wearing. The bad news is that zoos and aquariums remain perennial popular weekend favorites, so crowds can clog the fences and surround the cages. The Monterey Bay Aquarium has not just densely packed schools of fish, but even denser packed schools of humanity almost every single day it's open. Be prepared to move slowly, and to thread through the herd of humanity to find the restrooms (which will probably have lines snaking out the doors) and slightly lower traffic areas to whip out your stool for a rest. To avoid the worst of the crowds, pick an off-season weekday afternoon for your trip to the zoo. Or find one of the smaller local zoos, where the crowds never get quite so staggering but the animals still parade for the pleasure of the watching hairless mammals.

Whether you'll find reasonable access to food and drink varies widely depending on your zoo of choice, but expect it to be on the stingy side—zoos concentrate on feeding the animals, not the people. The biggies tend to have some concessions, but if you have any specific dietary needs at all, bring your own snacks. A bottle of water will quickly become your best friend on merciless sunny summer days out at the zoo, as water fountains will be few and far between, and of questionable quality.

Planned Amusement: Theme Parks

<u>Disneyland and Disneyworld</u>

I love Disneyland, even though I probably shouldn't. They must spray some sort of happiness-inducing chemical into the air inside the park that makes nearly everyone feel the pull of joy despite the ultra-super-hyper-aggressive marketing and in-your-face-and-all-open-orifices sales that crowd every square inch of the park.

But to face a full day at a sprawling amusement park, I need to think first and buy my $100+ Park Hopper Pass later. What with the chronic pain that's often exacerbated by too much walking and standing in lines, and the chronic fatigue that…er, makes me tired, one of those power scooter things starts to look appealing.

And as always, are there enough clean bathrooms to go around, especially during crowded weekends and holidays?

Taking a Load Off

Finding a place to sit down can be tough—you may find yourself attempting to park it on a concrete flower box, then being chased off by security. Avoid parades, and plan stops in restaurants and cafes for (almost) guaranteed seats several times each day.

The Bathroom Ride

Cleanliness and availability of necessary facilities–those all-important bathroom rides that you'll visit more than any other attraction–are strong points at Disneyland. Uncle Walt apparently thought the "needs of a big crowd" thing through properly when designing his first park, and it shows in restroom design. They've got adequate stalls to handle crowds, plenty of sinks, baby-changing stations, and an in-out traffic flow pattern that minimizes people tripping over one another. Even in high season, lines in the ladies rooms rarely last more than a few minutes. No restful seating, sadly. But janitors keep the restrooms clean at almost all times.

Keep that park map they gave you handy, otherwise the well-placed but attractively camouflaged bathrooms might be tough to find in an urgent situation.

Remaining Seated Throughout the Park

This web page has great info for folks with mobility problems who want to visit Disneyland:

http://www.disneymouselinks.com/Disneyland-Disabilities.aspx

It's got info on which rides are accessible (answer: most of them), and how much scooter and wheelchair rentals cost inside the park. In 2009, it's $65/day for a scooter/ECV and $35/day for a wheelchair. The site also offers links to outside vendors of rentable scooters, most of which are cheaper than renting at Disneyland.

Random Tip

The FastPass thing that's offered on the popular rides works really well for me. I can get my FastPass for a ride, and then go do something else until my time slot comes up. Like *sit the bleep down* for 20-30 minutes if I need a break.

I've done this, and then discovered that all my perfectly healthy companions have joined me for a FastPass and a drink and a load off their feet. Apparently, following me around makes a day in Disney less exhausting for the non-disabled folks—I create an "excuse" to keep them from overdoing it with the running around and not eating/drinking enough and standing in overlong lines. Who knew?

Other Theme Parks

Amusement parks exhaust even the healthiest of teenagers. Granted, the teens tend to run around and scream, which takes more energy than walking sedately. But still—think hard about your priorities for your trip before deciding to tackle a theme park. Of course, if your kids have demanded roller coasters and you've promised, you've gotta do what you've gotta do.

Planning a day or three in advance has never been more vital than before you go to an amusement park. If you've ever even thought about needing mobility assistance, arrange for it. It will be more than worth the money and hassle. Pack as though you're going to war—prepare a day pack with water bottle, healthy and hearty snacks, hat, sunscreen, hand sanitizer, cell phone, extra battery for your cell phone, extra pain meds, all your other daytime and evening meds, folding stool (if you're not going with a scooter or a chair), and everything your family will need. Then make somebody else (preferably one of those healthy kids) carry it as much as possible. Kids carry the pack while walking; you keep a hold of it while they're on the rides makes for a decent division of labor.

Beware of fairs. Especially big county and state fairs. These might sound like reasonable things for travelers with pain to visit. Certainly the title "county fair" evokes a small, down-home vision of shambling walks past prize pumpkins, perhaps sitting alongside a happy crowd of square dancers as the sun sets gently in the west.

In reality, fairs contain crowds of people and require walking for deceptive distances. There are few seats available unless you carry your own folding stool or chair. Food for sale at fairs never seems to be made with those gorgeous blue-ribbon veggies and fruits on display. Instead you're stuck with delicious but nutrition-free cotton candies and funnel cakes—not the kind of sustenance that adequately fuels a traveler with pain on a long day of walking interspersed with standing in lines and riding the tilt-a-whirls and other carnival rides.

If you go to a fair, go with a plan—don't just wander aimlessly. Bring that folding stool and some healthy snacks too. Pick up a map of the fair at the entrance gates, and plot your route so you can see the things you're interested in and skip those that won't thrill you or your family. Stop to rest oftener than you think you need to. Take advantage of sit-down stuff like the concerts that often run all day at fairs, the horse racing, or the animal demonstrations.

Water Parks

Water parks like Raging Waters have facilities for handicapped visitors because the law says they must. But the truth is that water parks are for healthy people. Young healthy people who can walk and run and swim and slip and fall on the faux-rock pathways without serious consequences. Being able to survive a second-degree sunburn helps too, because there's no such thing as a sunscreen that holds up to the abuse heaped upon it by the environment of a water park. You've got to reapply it every hour or you're going to fry.

If you absolutely must visit a waterslide park, plan to spend most of your time out on the scrubby lawns or concrete patios such places provide. Bring a folding chaise lounge and a beach umbrella as well as your amusement-park survival kit, but make somebody else carry it into the park for you. Expect to have to unpack some of it for gate security.

To avoid as much misery as you can, buy your tickets in advance and get to the park early. That way you'll deal with the least of the entrance lines, and you'll have a better choice of shady spots on which to plant your flag and secure your territory for the day.

Water park food is almost uniformly awful—think steamed hamburgers and microwaved frozen pizza. And they often won't let you bring your own food or drink in. Check the policies of the park before you go. And if you need to, bring a small cooler and leave it in the trunk of your car, then use the in-out hand stamp policy most water parks have to go out to the parking lot to eat a decent meal.

Chapter 6: Outdoor Adventures

You Don't Actually Need to Climb Every Mountain or Ford Every Stream

I love the outdoors—I wish I could be one of those adventure travelers who goes out to conquer the back country with only a tiny tent and dried meals. But I can't, because my body won't tolerate that sort of abuse. And yet, I'm not willing to condemn myself to indoor-only vacations. Such a huge part of the joy of traveling is experiencing new environments, whether that's a five-mile stroll in an urban jungle or surfing lessons on a tropical beach.

So I've found ways to enjoy the out-of-doors without kicking myself into a pain flare.

Hiking: Walking by Another Name

Hiking is walking on dirt, no more and no less. If you can walk, you can hike. You just need to choose your trails carefully. That means, as always, planning ahead, even if it's only 15 minutes ahead.

Don't just pull the car over to the side of the road when you see a trail head sign, hop out, and take off with no knowledge of the terrain. That trick can be dangerous, even for a perfectly healthy traveler. For a traveler with pain, it can be disastrous.

Instead, get a trail map. For unincorporated wilderness areas, you'll need to grab a map from the Internet before you arrive. If you're in a state or national park, your best bet is to stop at a Visitors Center before you start out on any hike. Not only will you get a map of the local trail system, you can talk to rangers about the trails you're interested in tackling. The rangers are always your best source of information, and many of them absolutely love to talk about their parks. Explain your limits—you can walk no more than a mile, or you must stay on flat ground, or you need to sit down every couple hundred feet—and ask which will be the best trails for you.

If you're looking at a map on your own, the most important place to start is length of trails. Be sure, as you're reading the map, that you're looking at distance *round trip*--not all trail maps use round-trip distances so you may have to do your own math. Next, look at the vertical gain or loss of the trails—this will tell you how much climbing you'll have to do. Don't be deceived—downhill can be much more difficult than uphill, especially with already tired leg muscles.

Interpretive trails and nature trails are great for travelers with pain. These trails are usually short and flat, with lots of signs describing the flora and fauna and other nearby natural features. Any trails that are described as paved, boardwalked, or accessible to wheelchairs tend to be good for travelers with pain too—but not always. Be sure to look at the length of the trail, even if it's "improved," and check or ask if there are stairs and if so how many!

Water Recreation: Dive In!

Oceans, lakes, rivers, creeks, and ponds—no natural feature draws tourism like a body of water. While the best view of a waterfall tends to be from the dry land nearby, much of the wealth of water we come upon in our travels tempts us to dive in.

I'm a sucker for water—I grew up spending my summers at my family's tumble-down lake cabin in the woods of Eastern Washington. My mom nearly had to float dinner out onto the water for me; I was so uninterested in getting out each evening.

With chronic pain, what water sports will make a splash, and which will sink like rocks?

As always, how athletic you can be depends on your current state of health, past experience, physical endurance, and muscular strength. And your doctor's recommendation, of course.

If your doctor has okayed it, soaking in the hotel's hot tub makes for a wonderful way to diminish pain.

On the other hand, class 5 whitewater rafting, wakeboarding, big-wave surfing, and kite-boarding will probably cripple you if they don't kill you.

Playing in the Snow

Downhill skiing and snowboarding may be the ultimate sports for healthy people. Careening down a frozen mountainside with one or two fiberglass strips tied to your feet will play hell with whatever chronic or acute pain condition you've got.

XC (the hip name for cross-country) means plodding uphill with skis on your feet as well as sliding down sometimes steep grades. XCers can glide well off the beaten path too, though beginners do better sticking to groomed and patrolled trails.

If you were an avid skier, XCer, or snowshoer before you became a chronic pain patient, you've got a leg up—including muscle memory. Just plan carefully before you hit the slopes or the trails. Remember that you may not have the endurance or muscular strength you were accustomed to. If your physical condition permits, embark on a conditioning program a few weeks before your trip. Work your leg strength and your cardio, so you'll be in the best shape possible. Then plan to be able to ski less than you were accustomed to before the pain. That might mean less time on the slopes or trails, it might mean choosing easier slopes, and it might mean both.

Emotion and ego can take a hit if you must downgrade from double-black to blue, dawn patrol to half-day in the afternoon. So ask yourself which you'd prefer--being out on the trails with the wind in your hair? Or sitting at home, watching daytime TV again, some more? I'd rather have half an hour out on the slopes and the great feeling of being outside doing something fun.

Are snow sports are an all new adventure for you? Step 1: book a lesson! Even for snowshoeing, find a class or a guided walk with a competent instructor who can help you and a group of folks who will be slogging along nearby.

Don't expect to be able to ski/board/shoe every day of your winter vacation. Depending on your condition, plan one day out, one day inside with your feet up. Or one day out, two days in, with the day out meaning four hours, two hours…whatever you can reasonably manage without pushing yourself into a pain flare.

That means that the weeklong lift passes won't save you money. Instead, buy lift tickets on a day-to-day basis. Equipment may still be cheaper if you rent it for the duration of your trip, and you'll have the advantage of acclimating to the boots and boards, which can make paying for the downtime worth it.

Find a place to play that's got warmth and seating nearby. Classic ski lodges have the best setups—you can go into the lodge still wearing your ski boots. Benches and chairs abound, and they sell coffee and hot cocoa. The fancy lodges sometimes even have couches.

Beware of kiddie snow play activities like sledding and snowball fights. Especially the sledding and saucer rides. No question—it's super-fun to slide down a snowy hillside on a slab of plastic at any age. But climbing back up that hill over and over again gets super-tiring fast, and that fatigue can be deceptive. When you head out to play with your kids or your friends, keep your physical state in mind and when you need to rest, rest. If you're driving out to a sledding or snow-play area, pack more than the plastic saucer and the ski cap. Also bring folding chairs, a thermos or two filled with your favorite hot beverage, and extra blankets to wrap up in.

Come to think of it, stash an extra blanket and a cup of hot coffee someplace nearby whenever you plan to be out in the snow—even if the "recreation" is shoveling your own front walk.

National and State Parks

The United States has a wonderful National Park system, rife with opportunity for visitors with all kinds of disabilities to enjoy the country's best scenery.

The best first stop in any national park is the visitor's center. Here's where you grab a map and find a friendly ranger to chat with. National park rangers are friendly creatures, easy to approach, and often starved for people to talk to. Get a good ranger talking, and you'll learn everything you need to know about hiking trails that suit your personal physical ability, the best places to tour in your car, and where the fish are biting this season. Rangers will also cheerfully tell you which dirt roads aren't so safe for two-wheel-drive cars, how to avoid flash-flooding zones, and what kind of safety gear you'll need for outdoor adventures. Pay special attention if a ranger tells you to avoid a certain road, trail, or region—she's not just enjoying the sound of her own voice. She honestly doesn't want to have to try to pull you out of a bad situation.

Many national parks have wonderful campgrounds, some have hotels, and some don't permit people to sleep within their borders. If you want to stay within the bounds of a national park, you will need to (sing it with me) plan your trip in advance. In season (summertime, for all but the desert national parks of the Southwest and California), campsites and lodge rooms are often booked solid for months in advance. Many national parks maintain a certain number of first-come, first-camped only campgrounds, but you need to know where these are and show up early in the morning to get yourself a space. For travelers with pain, I recommend minimizing the stress of not knowing where you're going to sleep at night and making advanced reservations.

Just because it's a National Park, doesn't mean that you're going to Disneyland. Plenty of National Parks, especially those in the West, include a lot of undeveloped, wild, and frankly dangerous territory. Do NOT expect services such as gas, food, restrooms, and pharmacies to pop up every few miles in every national park. Animals won't be tame, waters won't be protected by lifeguards, and visitors are expected to arrive prepared. Death Valley, for example, has precisely zero 24-hour restaurants, supermarkets, or pharmacies. The Valley boasts two gas stations total and almost no cell phone service at all. Plus it's got super-hot temperatures, no cities within 50 miles, and tons of dirt roads that sometimes exude tire-shredding volcanic glass for no good reason. All that said,

Death Valley's stunning beauty is more than worth the extra effort it takes to see it in safety and comfort.

For the best, comfiest, safest National Park visit you can take, research in advance to find what you'll need in your park of choice. The National Park Service's web site, www.nps.gov, is surprisingly useful for a government site—you can get info on everything from lodgings to hiking trails to in-park safety.

The National Park Service offers some fabulous passes. Currently, they're all under the name America the Beautiful – National Parks and Federal Recreational Land Pass. The Senior Pass, available to any US citizen or permanent resident over the age of 62, grants lifetime access to any National Park (plus several other types of recreational land, plus interesting discounts) for the fantastic one-time cost of $10.

For people whose disabilities are permanent, the Access Pass offers free lifetime access to National Parks and federal recreational lands. To get this pass, bring your documentation to a National park to receive the pass in person. Documentation can be a doctor's letter, SSDI or SSI income proof, or a document from a state vocational rehab program.

And finally, for the rest of us—the Annual Pass costs $80 per year and permits access to all Parks and most federal recreation land. If you're planning to visit more than three National Parks in a single year, the Pass pays for itself.

By the time this book is printed, prices and programs may have changed. Check the NPS site for the latest and greatest information about National Parks Passes:

https://pwrcms.nps.gov/pwr/fees_passes.htm

State park quality and amenities vary widely, often by state. Hee! But seriously, a state park can be anything from thousands of acres of forest complete with campgrounds, cabins, and convenience stores to a historic park centered around a Civil War battlefield that hosts re-enactors every weekend to a deserted stretch of beach with a gravel parking lot.

A near-to-home state park can make a great one or two-day "test run trip" if you haven't been able to travel in a while. Pick a park that features activities you think you'd like to try—hiking, fishing, beachcombing, swimming, kite-flying, bird watching, overnight camping. Make sure that your chosen park is within a comfortable driving range of your house—probably no more than an hour away. Do a few minutes of preliminary research on the park before you go, so that you can pack appropriately for the environment, just as you would on an overnight trip. That might mean anything from a sweatshirt in case it's cool, to a swimsuit and towel, to a cooler stocked with food and drink if the park doesn't have easily accessible concessions. Remember to bring your meds (enough for twice as long as you plan to be away from home), phone numbers, and extra cash for emergencies. Consider packing a first-aid kit, a comfy folding chair or chaise lounge, and a pillow and blanket in case you find yourself wanting a nap.

Drive on out to the park and enjoy! Do a few of the things that look fun—even to the point of pushing your usual limits just a little bit. Let yourself take a hike or go for a swim. Pay attention to how you feel while you're out at the park, during the drive home, and the following day. You'll have a decent gauge for your body's response to a day out on a longer vacation.

As always, the trick to enjoying a trip to a state park is to know what you're getting into before you go. Most state park systems have websites (of varying quality and utility)—a good place to start when you're looking for amenities like food shops, bathrooms, running water, accessible trails, and parking lots. Not all state parks have all these things, so be aware and be prepared before you go, especially if you're planning a multi-day visit.

Most state parks cost a little bit less to enter than national parks do, but expect at least a nominal entrance or parking fee. And expect to pay that fee in cash rather than by credit card. Campsites almost always cost extra; as the Great Recession continues, state park campgrounds, cabins, and lodges are enjoying a renaissance as an affordable alternative to higher-priced hotels. That means that wanna-be park patrons need to book early, especially for the popular parks during peak season. Rolling into a popular park's beachside campground at 5pm on Friday in July, thinking you're going to get a great campsite near the restrooms with a shade tree is a sure road to disappointment, angst, and likely a lot more driving than you intended for the day.

Chapter 7: Shopping

Choosing Where and When To Shop, Not Just What to Buy

Shopping costs more than just money, it costs time and energy. When you're traveling, time and especially energy are at a premium. So choose wisely—not about what to buy (that's the next section) but about where and when and how to shop.

Think about skipping your destination's mall if you've got a similar mall with similar stores in it at home. Same goes for outlet centers. A few exceptions to this suggestion include shopping centers that differ significantly from your home shopping turf, a trip specifically for shopping at an outlet mall, and Oregon. Oregon has no sales tax.

On a non-shopping trip, plan time to shop without going overboard. Take your condition into account—can you walk for an hour with frequent stops to examine merchandise? Can you stand in long register lines at popular stores? Can you tolerate lack of access to bathrooms, food, and places to sit down? Do crowds stress you out?

If you can only shop for a few minutes at a time, pick out the most unique, memorable, or meaningful places to peruse merchandise in the region you're visiting. Visit a shop you can't find at home if you've only got a few minutes; a local marketplace or bazaar if you can spend several hours.

In some regions, shopping can be a major tourist activity. In Morocco or Turkey, it would be a bummer not to plan a whole day to explore the outdoor bazaars. And in the Napa or Sonoma wine regions of California, the main point of visiting is to taste and collect local vintages, many of which are produced in such small quantities that they can't even be bought on the Internet.

Hawaiian goods like macadamia nuts and Kona coffee can be bought elsewhere, true. But they cost far less and come in a much wider variety in shops on the islands.

Practicing Physically Necessary Restraint: Sure that chainsaw sculpture looks great, but can you carry it across the airport in a tote bag?

For reasons I still don't comprehend, my mom once bought a chainsaw sculpture of a cat while on a trip through the Northern California redwood forest region. She had the good sense to have it shipped home, but still—why?

Ask yourself 'why' before you buy anything big or preposterous when you're on the road. Do you really need a chainsaw sculpture or a glass coffee table shaped like an octopus? How about that tacky souvenir coconut cup that makes the drink cost an extra $10—do you really think you'll use it once you're back home? This question can keep you from spending precious cash and valuable energy lugging home something you don't need and might not even want after a month back home.

After the why, ask yourself 'where' squared. That is, where will it go when you get it home, and more important, where will you pack it to get it home? If you're traveling by air, train, or bus, the stuff you buy has to fit in your luggage. And excess luggage ain't so cheap as it used to be, especially on airplanes. Shipping things home can be a viable alternative (and necessary if you've purchased that glass octopus table), though shipping costs money too.

More even than extra money, consider the physical toll that your purchases will exact on your body. The more pounds of stuff you buy, the more pounds of stuff you carry. Many folks with chronic pain can't lug 50 pounds worth of shopping bags hundreds of yards, days in a row. Even if it's packed in your suitcases, you'll have to lift it at some point.

If you're on a road trip you might have more room to stash your new treasures. But not infinite room. If your pain condition requires that you be able to recline your seat all the way back at times, or to lie down in the back, you can't fill that space with the results of shopping gone awry.

Tacky Tiki souvenirs that are actually made in China line the tables at hundreds of garage sales across the Mainland each year. For that matter, ticky-tacky souvenirs always seem to end up crowding the shelves in secondhand shops and piling up in landfills. Think about wasting less time shopping for vinyl snow globes and hula girls; instead seek out genuine unusual goods that your friends will actually enjoy and maybe even keep.

Chapter 8: Night Life -
You Can Dance If You Want To

Clubbing
Not for the faint of heart (or legs, or eardrums)

Clubbing costs a lot of energy, even at home. It's not just the dancing—actually, dancing is the fun part. But clubbing takes so much more effort than that. First you've got to get to the club. In LA and San Francisco, that means finding a parking space. In Manhattan, it means grabbing a cab or taking a subway ride.

If it's a hip club, next comes the waiting in line. That doesn't take so long if you're a pretty young woman or a rock star; if you're male or unfamous you may be standing outside in questionable weather for over an hour.

Once you're in, you get to thread through the crush of humanity to...more crush of humanity. There's no such thing as "average seating" in nightclubs. Some clubs have whole rooms furnished with squishy secondhand sofas, plus plenty of barstools and benches and other places where weary dancers can cop a squat. Other clubs have six sticky hard stools for three hundred patrons. The only way I know of to guarantee seating in a high end nightclub is to reserve a table for bottle service. That means that for the low, low price of about $500-$1,000 for a bottle of booze worth about $50 at the grocery store around the corner, you and your friends get a table and a waitperson for the evening. If you happen to be a zillionaire, go for it!

The restroom situation in the clubs tends to run from mediocre to dismal. I've been to clubs that boast one filthy toilet in a closet for their female patrons. A female friend once spent an uncomfortable evening in another club, wherein the ladies room line was forced to snake out onto a catwalk, allowing the "gentlemen" in the establishment to look up the women's skirts. Yuck.

But for some travelers, the opportunity to hit the hippest night spot may be the highlight of the whole trip. So if spending the night at the trendiest club is your heart's desire, go for it. Just plan carefully, and be aware of the pitfalls. Check out your destination in advance, online at a bare minimum. If possible, stop by the club during the daytime and see if they'll let you in to look at the bathrooms and seating, sniff the air, peek at the sound system, and maybe even ask the employees a few questions about what it's like at night. If you can't get in the door, call on the phone and ask about all this stuff.

Do whatever you can to avoid standing in line to gain entrance to the club. The super-spendy bottle/table service reservations will get you right on in. For the less affluent clubgoer, many night spots have "lists" online that you can jump onto—then when you arrive, you give your name to the gatekeeper and get in before the people in the regular line.

On clubbing day, take it easy. Instead of an afternoon hike, take an afternoon nap. Eat good meals, including a hearty dinner, but hold off on the adult beverages until you're out at your nighttime destination. Do take your meds on schedule; in fact, consider taking any evening meds before you head out to party. And once you're there, moderate your liquor consumption. Or at least pace yourself—getting plowed in order to dull your pain so you can dance harder or stay out later might seem like a good idea, but it's got some obvious flaws. Hangovers do not ameliorate chronic pain, especially chronic pain that's been heightened by a night out. But speaking of that, plan for an easy, laid-back, nap-filled day on the day after your club night too.

The Bar Scene

Bars, the easier-going cousins of clubs, run from local dives to totted-up tourist traps. It's easy enough to check out a bar or two when you're traveling with chronic pain, and it's a good way to get a feel for the local night life in most urban destinations. Just be aware of the usual characteristics of bars—in many states, cigarette smoking is still permitted and the haze can get thick. Bars, by their nature, get noisy as the night goes on—especially when there's live music or karaoke. Bathrooms in bars often resemble crosses between toxic waste spills and swamps.

For best results, show up at your chosen bar an hour or two earlier than fashionable. That way you're much more likely to get a table or a barstool—by the way, chilling at a table is usually more comfortable than bellying up to the bar itself. And as contrary as it might seem, try to drink as little liquor as possible. Remember, you're on the road, which is already stressing your body. Alcohol adds to that stress, and can push you over the line into a pain flare.

BYO toilet paper or extra tissues. Can't hurt, might save your whole night.

Live Theater, Music, and Comedy
Uncomfortable seats, bad drinks, restricted views, long restroom lines—what's not to love?

Live entertainment can be a big part of enjoying a destination—who journeys all the way to New York City and doesn't want to see a show on Broadway? Visitors to Vegas often shell out $200 per ticket to see shows every night of their stay. And heck, there's something special about journeying to a friend's hometown to see him perform stand-up comedy on open-mic night at the local bar.

The most important question to ask about any show you'd like to see is simple: Can I leave in the middle if my pain spikes suddenly? If you sit on the aisle at a mall movie theater, it's easy enough to slip out if you're not feeling well, even in the midst of intense action on the screen. But if you're seated dead-center of the orchestra section in a Broadway theater and your pain starts bothering you right after the first intermission, it may be harder to bail. At the very least, it will *feel* harder to leave in that kind of situation. And it will be harder physically—you'll be squeezing sideways past annoyed people, tripping over feet and handbags in the dark. If that sounds like more than you can usually handle, think twice before splurging on "the best seats in the house" to the latest hit Broadway musical.

Some live entertainment is more difficult for travelers with pain than others. In my opinion, the toughest types of live shows with pain are rock concerts and big Broadway productions. These events tend to have the biggest crowds, most difficult to navigate seating arrangements, sparsest bathroom facilities, and furthest-away parking lots. Outdoor theaters also present a thorny set of problems, including temperature fluctuations and seating (dis)comfort issues. The easiest live shows to enjoy usually appear in smaller venues—comedy clubs, small theaters, dinner theaters. Chairs in these kinds of clubs can be wretchedly uncomfortable, true. But it's easier to get up and walk around if you need to. It's also easier to get up and *leave* if you're really feeling poorly.

Pick one or two shows or concerts you want to attend at your destination. When I'm traveling, I try to choose live events that I can't see at home or specific venues that are special. To me, it's worth it to see a play on Broadway in an actual Broadway playhouse. On the other hand, I'd rather check out a quirky little production of a locally written play in Toronto than go to a stadium rock concert that will be coming to my hometown six months later.

Other people might advise you to always go for a matinee or the earliest possible show. Not me. I say, know your own body's rhythms and pick show times when you'll feel energetic and as physically good as possible. That might be the late show rather than the matinee. I like to take a nice long nap in the afternoon, then enjoy a leisurely dinner, then take in a later show. Because I'm a night owl by nature, this schedule works well for me.

When you buy tickets for a show, forgo those great seats in the middle of the row and find something as close to the aisle as you can get. If the theater you'll be at has a map online, check it out before your trip. Find your seats, and then find where the entrances and exits and restrooms are in relation to those seats. Also check for public spaces—lobbies and lounges and hallways—where you might be able to sit down and rest, or even lie down if you needed to. Keep that map with you when you go to the show, or use the one that's often in the program someplace. Stash a small

penlight on your person someplace, just in case you need to read
your map in the dark. (But try not to use it during anything but a
rock show.) Wear comfortable shoes, even if you're female. You
may end up walking further than you want to. Dress in layers. For
indoor theater, a jacket or wrap works well. On trips to outdoor
theaters, don't hesitate to wear a sleeveless shirt under a down coat
and carry a fleece blanket and a flask of hot tea. Try to avoid
seatless venues, especially indoor seatless concerts. Nothing's less
comfortable. At least at outdoor seating-free shows, you can usually
bring in your own beach chairs with backs. Avoid sitting near the
sound system at concerts, for the obvious eardrum comforting
reasons.

Know that if you're going to Coachella or frankly any rock
concert, there will be smells. People around you will be
surreptitiously smoking, whether posted signs forbid it or not.
That's the nature and culture of rock concerts, and I don't
recommend trying to change your fellow attendees' attitudes.

Expect the restroom situation to lie somewhere between
challenging and abysmal on a scale of 1 to 10; it's always worse for
the women than for the men. Go right before you take your seat
just before the show starts, always. The only way I know to get to
the bathroom ahead of the stampeding herd at intermission is to
know that intermission is coming, have an aisle seat already, bolt for
the aisle at the exact instant that intermission begins, and run like
hell. This is just as true for opening night at the opera as it is for a
college black-box play, or for a Green Day show.

Especially if your health isn't great, plan to do little else on
"show day" other than go to your show. That might mean spending
the day lounging in your hotel, reading or watching TV and
napping during the day. It might even include ordering room
service or getting take-out for lunch and dinner rather than going
out to a sit-down restaurant. So be it; resting up for the day makes
it much more likely that you'll be able to really relax, sit back, and
enjoy the show.

Chapter 9: Using the Euphemism - We've All Got to Go Sometime

Finding the Nearest Restroom, Wherever You Are

No matter who you are, no matter what your health, no matter where you're traveling, at some point you'll need to find a bathroom. Needing a toilet is the great human equalizer.

The universal low-tech approach to finding a public restroom is to look for signs. Wherever you're going, be sure you know how they sign their public restrooms and what the words and pictures they use look like (even if you know no other words in the language).

Some places—like Disneyland—put out maps with the location of restrooms on them. Get as many of those sorts of maps as possible. Study the map before you need the restrooms, to get familiar with where they're located.

Nowadays, high-tech ways to find a bathroom in an unfamiliar region have popped up in the iThings universe. SitorSquat was the first find-a-crapper app to take the iPhone world by storm. I've tried SitorSquat in the continental US and it's worked like a charm for me. I haven't yet tried it off-continent, so your mileage may vary. SitorSquat works on iPhones and iPod Touch (of course), Blackberry, via text message, and on the Internet (laptop or desktop computers).

A newcomer to the world of toilet-finding apps is Have2P. I have no personal knowledge of this one. Have2P works on iPhone, iPod Touch, and Android devices, and has the dubious "feature" of starting a fresh search for restrooms when it feels you (read: the phone) shaking.

Want to try one of the iPhone apps? Check out their features at www.sitorsquat.com and www.have2p.com. Download either or both of them from the iPhone Apps store, which is part of the ubiquitous iTunes. Be aware that you'll need to sign up when you first access www.iTunes.com and they'll ask for a credit card number **before** they'll let you start shopping.

Problem Facilities

Issues with international toilets, filth, broken johns, other unbearable conditions, and how to surmount them

If you're traveling outside of your cultural comfort zone, be aware that the toilet facilities may not be what you're used to at home. While knowing that things may be different, difficult, or disgusting won't fix the facilities, it can keep away an unpleasant sense of shock when you find yourself confronting a stinking hole in the ground with no instructions posted about how to go about…going.

First step to making it work, bathroom wise, is to BYO TP. You can't go wrong keeping a small packet of tissues in your purse or your pocket whenever you leave home. Worst case—you don't need the tissues and you've carried an extra ½ ounce around. The further you travel, the more toilet paper can be necessary. I usually keep a roll in my car, even when I'm not on a road trip. And I'd slip a roll or two into my suitcase if I were headed someplace like India, China, Egypt, or Mexico.

It's super simple to carry some hand sanitizer as well. I like the spray on organic lavender stuff, but any small bottle will do the job.

If your medical condition requires that you use the bathroom often, prepare for that when you're planning to travel. Preparing might mean getting maps of your urban destinations that include public restrooms. Or it might mean picking up a few portable urinals to carry with you on a road trip that's taking you to a rural region with restrooms few and far between. It may even mean wrapping your head around the concept of wearing adult diapers in certain situations. Only you can know your digestive system's needs and vagaries, how long you can wait, and what kind of pain you'll endure if you have to hold it.

Finally, if you're traveling abroad, research the realities of the restrooms at your destination. Toilet facilities are not universal by any means. Wherever you're headed, use the Internet to find photos of a typical toilet. Know that you may not be able to sit down—you may be expected to squat over a hole instead. Even if you can sit, seat covers may be right out. Sanitation might be much better than at home, but more likely it will be worse. Sometimes far worse. But you'll still have to go sometime, despite the discomfort, smells, and possible pain.

It might seem silly or petty to base your travel destinations on the style of toilets available, but it's not. No one can avoid using the bathroom, and if you're not able to squat over a hole in the ground without inducing a pain flare, trying to travel to a place where you'll have to do that a dozen times a day will make you miserable. And there's no sense in traveling if you're going to be nothing but miserable.

Planes, Trains, and Automobiles
Bathrooms in transit

Oh, those ridiculous little cubicles that pass as restrooms (emphatically without the "rest" part) in airplanes, on trains, and in buses. Well, at least they exist. Yippee.

I doubt I need to explain that transit restrooms are usually tiny, often dirty, and may contain little more than the most basic of necessities (the toilet). To enhance your comfort, bring your own amenities—toilet paper, tissues, and hand sanitizer.

When you've got to use the bathroom on a vehicle, timing is everything. Specifically, timing the need to go so that you don't end up in a line with everyone else in whatever fast-rattling tin can you're sitting in. Try to use the bathroom before any meal service; everyone else will find that they need to go soon after they finish eating and drinking. On planes, you've got to dodge the drink carts of course, but if you can stand for a length of time you can wait in one of the vestibules and at least look at a different part of the plane for a while.

Trains have the advantage of multiple restrooms in each car; in an emergent restroom need, you can brave the rocking and use another car's facilities. On the bus, sadly, there's one bathroom and if it's in use, it's in use. I try to use the restroom on the bus whenever it's free and I have even the smallest need, so that I don't wind up cross-legged and whimpering while someone else seems to be trying to finish War and Peace in there.

The bottom line: go early, go late, go whenever you can.

Chapter 10: Resting Up

Go To Bed Early or Sleep Late (or Both!)

The single most important thing you'll do when you're traveling is **sleep**. When you're sleeping, your body heals and prepares itself for your next day's adventures.

I recommend keeping as close to your regular daily schedule as you can while you're on your trip. But that's easier for me to say than for travelers to achieve. Between noisy motel rooms, mattresses that resemble slabs of concrete, jet lag, and pre-dawn or post-midnight activities, it can seem nearly impossible to catch even a few zzzs, much less the eight-plus hours a traveler with pain needs.

I've developed all sorts of methods to cope with sleep disturbances on the road. I mix and match whichever techniques I need most (and can manage physically) on any given trip. Overall, the best thing you (and I) can do is to try to recreate my home sleep environment as closely as possible. Here's how:

1. Diminish Ambient Sound

I favor total silence when I sleep—not an easy commodity to come by in urban hotels, Interstate-side motels, or hostels. So I use **earplugs**. Yes, they took getting used to, but they work. If you're sensitive to sound when you sleep and you want to travel, start trying out different kinds of earplugs at home to find your favorite.

Other folks prefer soothing noises—music, water sounds, chirping birds. If that's your preference, download your favorite sounds to your iPod. If sleeping with ear buds doesn't work for you, look into some sturdy mini-speakers. While a few high-end hotels now offer iPod docks, they're far from ubiquitous, so it's best to bring your own.

For a quieter atmosphere in general, ask for a room as far away from the street as possible in urban hotels. (These are popular rooms—you might not get your wish if you don't make reservations well in advance.) In family-friendly motels, try to get a room that's further away from the pool. This one's easier—most families with kids want to be close to the water. And yes, I'm going to say it…for a quiet night's rest, avoid hostels altogether.

2. Douse the light

Many people have trouble sleeping in well-lit places, which makes sleeping while traveling a challenge at times.

A sleep mask makes a handy portable room/cabin/airplane seat darkener. I don't love 'em, but I tolerate them on airplanes and trains. If you're particularly sensitive to light when sleeping, find one of those super-comfy silk sleep masks and start practicing wearing it at home. It's the only sure way to get a dark place to sleep.

Some motels and hotels invest in blackout curtains. I don't love these—they turn day into night, and mess up my circadian rhythms (such as they are). But they keep a room dark, if that's what you need. About every room in Vegas (and every other casino city) has blackouts. If you like blackout curtains, ask whether your chosen motel or hotel stocks these in their bedrooms.

While you're chatting about draperies, you might also ask for a room that's away from exterior lights. This is a long shot—the desk clerk may have no clue which rooms lie window-on to the sun.

And again it must be mentioned—if you prefer to sleep in the dark, or a certain light level, avoid hostels.

3. Enhance your comfort however you can.

Whatever it takes to make yourself as comfortable as possible when you sleep, do it. Ask for more pillows. If you can, bring your own pillow from home. Adjust the temperature of your sleeping area to whatever works for you. Pile on more blankets if you like the weight or the warmth, or throw off the covers if you like it cool. Bring along your vaporizer if you're accustomed to sleeping with one.

4. Keep time.

Find yourself a regular schedule and stick to it, even if it's not your usual schedule. I tend to be more active when I'm traveling, but I keep to a rhythm. No matter how exciting your destination, remember how much sleep you usually need and get it. Need a nap? Take one—you're on vacation! If you love the nightlife, go ahead and stay up until 2am. But plan to sleep in.

Healthy folks sometimes decide not to sleep much on vacation so they don't miss anything. That doesn't work too well with pain—miss sleep and you'll miss everything afterward. Trust me.

Oh, and avoid hostels. Really—scheduled sleeping in a dorm environment is just this side of impossible.

5. Use chemical sleep aids advisedly

Got a 'script for Ambien? A bottle of melatonin? Break that stuff out and don't be afraid to use it early and often. On travel is not the place to get squeamish about sleep meds. It's better to deal with the hangovers than to go for a night without sleep. That goes double if you've traveled far enough to have jet lag.

If you've ignored the 'no hostels' advice…bring a *big* bottle of sleep drugs. Just sayin'.

6. Jet lag…

Sucks. If you can, sleep through it. All that advice that healthy people spout about staying up until the evening at your destination, no matter how tired it makes you, then getting up again early in the local morning time no matter how tired it makes you… It's crap, it will make you feel terrible, and it will get your trip off to a bad start.

Instead, follow your body's dictates for your first couple of days. If that means collapsing into bed at 3pm and sleeping till noon the next day–do it. If it means getting up at 4am…do that. Whatever works best for you, and gets you the rest you need. On average, I lose 12-24 hours at the beginning of every long-distance trip I take. Knowing that, I plan my activities accordingly.

The good news–when I finally emerge from my long sleep, I'm rested, refreshed, and physically and mentally ready to enjoy myself.

Siesta
A Civilized Custom You Can Enjoy Anywhere

In some countries, the local custom is to have a relaxed sit-down lunch at around noon or one o'clock. Then, rather than try to overcome the food coma and get back to work, the country heads for the bedroom and naps for a couple of hours. Shops and offices tend to be shut from 2pm-4pm, then open again until at least 7pm and occasionally 9pm.

I love this custom. Siestas can help a traveler with pain recover from a morning out, then enjoy the afternoon and evening without feeling they've missed out on anything. A few countries that adhere to siesta customs include Spain, Italy, Greece, Malta, India, China, Vietnam, and a number of countries in Latin America.

Wherever I travel, I take the siesta custom with me. Yes, I do miss things when I nap in the afternoon here in the States. That's one of the realities I live with as a traveler with pain. But it makes my trips so much more successful when I take some down time after lunch. Even if I don't actually sleep, I go back to my room and lay down. I dim the lights and snooze or read or even just stare out of the window and daydream for a while. If I'm in pain, I find that this is a great time to take my pain meds and then rest while they're kicking in. The meds work best if I can do this.

After an hour or two, I rise and get myself a glass of water and a light snack. I find myself refreshed and ready to tackle dinner out and maybe even some evening entertainment or window shopping.

Every day of your trip that you possibly can, take an afternoon siesta. Even if you don't sleep, spend some horizontal time in a dimly lit room. Can't make it back to your hotel? Find a place to stretch out wherever you are. At the very least, do your level best to find a place to sit down and kick back with a book or a magazine for an hour—I've been known to read for ten minutes and then put the magazine over my face in that universal signal for "taking a nap, please leave me alone." Even my car can become my siesta refuge if I roll the windows down.

Enjoy your siesta—what's not to love about the sleepy luxury of taking an afternoon nap—then rise refreshed and ready for an evening out on the town.

Chapter 11: After the Trip—Recovery Time

It's customary in the United States to get home from a trip on Sunday and fling back into work first thing Monday morning. This is a tough gig even for a healthy person—not only the mental shift from vacation brain to home-and-work brain, but the physical reset from vacation activities to work, childcare, and other daily activities.

When you schedule your trip, plan to spend between 10%-25% of your total vacation time kicking back at home afterwards. That means:

- Two-day weekend away – 4-6 hours after-trip rest
- One week away – 1-2 days after-trip rest
- Two weeks away – 1.5-3 days after-trip rest

That may mean that you'll have to cut the "away" part of your trip short so that you've got enough time to rest before returning to work or to your regular day-to-day life. I know I'm always tempted not to do this—I'd rather spend more time out on the road and I try to talk myself into believing that I won't need that much time to recover after my trips. But I always do need that time, and I've learned over the years to schedule accordingly.

When you're resting and recuperating, the key is rest. Sleep an hour or three more than you usually would each night. Finish that novel you started while you were on the plane home. Catch up on your favorite TV shows, stack your Netflix queue with your favorite movies, order a pizza…kick back and really take it easy. Listen to your body, and put its needs first. If you can't unpack your suitcases in one fell swoop, do it gradually, lifting and bending only a very little each day.

The after-trip rest period is also a great time to post photos of your vacation on Facebook or Flickr and order prints, and finish up a travel journal. In that journal, you might write down what worked and what didn't work on this trip with your pain. That information will help you to do even better when you start planning that next vacation…

Appendix: Additional Resources

A few favored books and websites that can help travelers with chronic pain

Know that while I'm listing a lot of resources here, I'm not specifically endorsing or recommending any of them.

Accessible Travel Web Sites

- Travels with Pain: http://travelswithpain.com
  The blog that inspired this book. I add new content at least once a week, often about specific destinations and activities.
- Barrier Free Travel: http://barrierfreetravels.com/serendipity/
  Candy Harrington's blog about the nuts and bolts of traveling with a disability. Primarily focused on wheelchair, scooter, and walker users.
- I-Can-Travel: http://www.i-can-travel.com
  Lots of links to accessible tour operators and lodgings around the world.
- Society for Accessible Travel and Hospitality: http://www.sath.org
  Web site of SaTH, a nonprofit organization dedicated to raising awareness of the needs of disabled travelers around the world.
- DisabledTravel.com: http://www.disabledtravelers.com/
  Accessible tour operators, travel companions for hire, home exchanges, other products and services for disabled travelers.
- Access-Able Travel Source: http://access-able.com
  Resources for disabled travelers; includes info for hearing and sight-impaired travelers as well as wheelchair-bound travelers.

Accessible Travel Books and Magazines

Almost every one of these books focuses on travel for people in wheelchairs or with other limited mobility problems rather than people with chronic pain and hidden disabilities. There's definitely some overlap in the needs of visibly disabled travelers and travelers with pain. So choose carefully, knowing that you may not be exactly the target audience for these books.

- 101 Accessible Vacations by Candy Harrington
  ISBN 1932603433 / 9781932603439
- Barrier-Free Travels by Candy Harrington.
  ISBN 1932603832 / 9781932603835
  http://barrierfreetravel.net/
- There *Is* Room at the Inn by Candy Harrington
  ISBN 1932603611 / 9781932603613
- Rick Steves Easy Access Europe
  ISBN-10: 1566919991
- How to Travel: A Guide for Persons With Disabilities by Fred Rosen
  ISBN-10: 1888725052
  ISBN-13: 978-1888725056
- Emerging Horizons:
  A travel magazine devoted to travelers with limited mobility.
  http://emerginghorizons.com/
  General Travel Guidebooks
  Pick your favorite travel guidebook series from among the many that crowd the bookshelves.
- Moon Handbooks
  A great series of general guidebooks to destinations around the world, except for Europe. Not disability-focused. Yes, I've written several Moon Handbooks to the state of California.
- Rick Steves
  The current super-favorite travel guides to Europe, written by genial TV star Rick Steves. Frankly, I hate the hand-drawn

maps. Other than that, I can't help but love these sweet, useful guides.

- AAA Lodging Guides
Available for free to AAA members, these comprehensive guides rate hotels, motels, inns, and lodges. Not disability-focused, but does note accessible features.